The Use of the Film

BASIL WRIGHT

ARNO PRESS & THE NEW YORK TIMES

New York · 1972

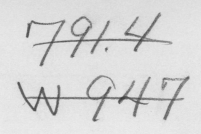
This volume was selected for
THE ARNO PRESS CINEMA PROGRAM
by George Amberg, Ph.D.,
Professor of Cinema,
New York University

Reprint Edition 1972 by Arno Press Inc.

Reprinted by permission of The Bodley Head Ltd.
Reprinted from a copy in The University of
   Illinois Library

LC# 75-169356
ISBN 0-405-03927-1

THE ARNO PRESS CINEMA PROGRAM
See last pages of this volume for titles.

Manufactured in the United States of America

NEW DEVELOPMENTS

The Use of the Film

NEW DEVELOPMENTS

1 THE ARTIST'S DILEMMA
2 MUSIC
3 BALLET
4 THE BOOK FRONT
5 THE THEATRE
6 THE USE OF THE FILM
7 EDUCATION FOR LIFE

[*other titles in preparation*]

Editorial Board

NEW DEVELOPMENTS

The Use of the Film

BASIL WRIGHT

A British Film Academy Recommendation

THE BODLEY HEAD   LONDON

First published 1948

Printed in Great Britain by
EATON PRESS, LIVERPOOL
for JOHN LANE THE BODLEY HEAD LTD.
8 Bury Place, London W.C.1

CONTENTS

FOREWORD   7

  I INDUSTRY AND ART   9
     Using Films. The New Art. Making films. The Camera.
     Editing. The Script. Sound. Music. It isn't so easy.
     Working in groups. How films get made. The com-
     mercial motive. The rise of the tycoons. Hollywood
     takes over. The all-powerful middleman. Protection.
     Rebirth of an Industry. The Vicious Circle. Ballyhoo.
     Problems of the box-office. The Virtuous Circle. What
     we want.

 II FANTASY AND FACT   33
     Beyond the box-office. Problems of patronage. Films
     are expensive. Technical problems. Where the money
     comes from. The bases of documentary. Pedagogics
     are not enough. Meeting a need. What documentary
     does. New audiences. The box-office of ideas. Films as
     a public service. New patrons. All sorts and conditions.
     Film Societies. Science stakes a claim. Children and
     Teachers. New films mean new methods. The Amateur.
     Will Hollywood cash in? The best of both worlds.

III WORLD CINEMA   54
     Screenspace for all. British bargaining points. The end
     of ballyhoo. Propaganda—real or unreal? 'Shop.'
     Brass tacks before Utopia. The biggest plan of all.

 IV BIBLIOGRAPHY   7

FOR PADDIE

FOREWORD

To John Grierson Esq.

Dear John,

You have often urged me to write a book. Now I have done so, if only on a very small scale. I have not the least doubt that you will tear it to bits, and I for one shall not blame you, if only because I know we both agree that books about films somehow manage to leave out all the fun and affection which make the film-world one of the more pleasant (and crazier) areas of operation.

Will you therefore read between the lines, and remember, as I do, the all-night sessions, the curious journeyings, the private and public jokes, the excursions into journalism (World Film News in particular), the sidelines of agricultural pursuits and *la vie sportive*, and all the other things you and I and the others have enjoyed in the process of trying to do a job of work (if I may quote your favourite phrase) in the cause of better films, better education, and better understanding between peoples.

Yours ever,

BASIL WRIGHT.

I. INDUSTRY AND ART.

T HE CINEMA has been described, by no means incorrectly, as the most important medium for the diffusion of human thought since the 15th century discovery of the printing press. The appeal of moving pictures is universal. As we sit in our local cinema seeing the big film, other people all over the world are seeing the same film (and ten to one it is an American film). But wherever it comes from it represents the plain fact that day and night, year in year out, the film is working on the thoughts and imagination of all sorts of people everywhere.

To us in Britain, as ordinary film-goers, the cinema means Hollywood films, British films, and 'unusual' continental films—in that order. We are not particularly aware, though we should be, that there are large and flourishing film industries in India, Egypt, South America. Indians and Arabs are some of the world's most assiduous film-fans, and they see films made for them by their own people as well as by the studios of the West.

It is easy, too, to accept the idea that the film is *par excellence* a form of entertainment. It is of course a fact that, as things are, the cinema has developed more along the lines of box-office than in any other direction. But by no means entirely.

Films have already been successfully used to teach Africans the principles of sanitation, hygiene, and the rotation of crops —to teach Basic English to Chinese students—to help combat tuberculosis and dysentry in Mexico.

All over the world films are used in schools and colleges, hospitals and training centres, villages (often in the open air), on street corners or in select metropolitan clubs, under all sorts of conditions—not merely to entertain, but for many other purposes, good, bad, and indifferent.

Thus—to take the analogy of the printing press—it is clear that just as books are not confined to novels of varying values, so the forms of filmic expression can (and should) be highly diverse. Conditioned as we are to the film novel or novelette, we tend to forget the possibilities and indeed the existence of film poems, film treatises, film reports, film textbooks and lectures, film sermons, film geographies, and film anthologies.

It is within a field as wide as this that any clear discussion of cinema should take place.

Using Films.

What then, are the bases from which the discussion can start? There are two. First, the means at the disposal of the film *maker*, and second the means at the disposal of the film *user*. I propose to start with the second point, because there is little interest in the making of films unless the makers know that the films are going to be seen.

People can use films for the following purposes :—

1. To enjoy several hours of imaginative, amusing, or soothing entertainment.

2. To receive an aesthetic pleasure of an order as high as that which can be obtained from works of art in other media.

3. To speculate with large sums of money (usually someone-else's).

4. To carry out political or other propaganda.

5. To advertise branded goods.

6. To record and preserve historical events.

7. To provide a public information service on matters affecting the community or sections of the community.

8. To instruct people in the use of machines, tools and weapons, and in the best methods of carrying out plans and operations.

9. To teach children in the classroom and students in the lecture hall, as an adjunct to the other means used by the teacher.

10. To provide a livelier background to the education of children and students by relating their school-work to the wider world for which their education is a preparation.

11. To educate and enlighten grown-up people in terms of general interest (e.g. public affairs) and of local and social interest.

12. To assist scientists and technicians of all sorts to keep abreast of new discoveries and technological developments, and to explain new processes and techniques.

13. To bring instruction, information and education to people who cannot read or write (some 65% of the world's population).

14. Finally, in all the ways listed above, to help peoples all over the world to understand each other and each other's problems, and so bring them closer together in the ways of peace.

To talk about cinema in this way may not be easy, but to me it is the only way which makes sense. It isn't easy, because cinema has grown up lopsided. It is worthwhile, because, however lopsidedly, the film has already proved its power over man's mind and heart and habit.

The New Art.

First, however, it is necessary to be clear about the first point I mentioned—the means at the disposal of the film-maker ; that is, the creative, expressive machinery of the film medium itself. A large number of books have been written on the art and technique of the film*, and to go into great detail here would be superfluous. I shall attempt no more than a brief summary.

Film is the only new art form developed by man since the dawn of history. All the other arts have grown with him since he first emerged as a creature capable of constructive thought and creative imagination.

The idea of making pictures move, is, of course, centuries old ; but its successful translation into practice had essentially to wait for the technological era which began with the industrial revolution. For cinema is the first and only art whose technique is the child of the laboratory and the machine.

The art of the film is indeed an apt and necessary phenomenon in this age of contracting spaces, concentrated populations, and complicated social and political organisations. It is a form of expression which, thanks to machines, to electricity, and to fast communications, can reach everyone everywhere at the same time.

* See Bibliography.

In earlier days all the people of a city like Athens could participate in the performance of dramas or comedies in their common theatre. Today the cinema, which can, if it wishes, achieve an aesthetic equal to that of any of the other arts, provides a similar means of participation to all the people of the world.

For, child of the machine age though it is, the cinema does, paradoxically, satisfy a deep, almost primitive desire in all of us—the desire to make pictures move. You can see this urge in the long history of painting. You can see it too in all young children who, as Jean Benoit Levy emphasises, are disconcerted by pictures which don't move, and try to convert them to movement by scribbling.* In this instinct they are at one with the caveman of prehistory. The invention of the cinema was, in a sense, the end of that quest for the capture of movement which began when the men of Altamira made their animal paintings on their cavern walls.

The film's illusion of movement is in itself psychologically satisfying ; and, despite the sound-track, it is on the pictorial that it relies for its magical appeal. When it ceases to be properly pictorial it ceases in proper terms to be a film. Incidentally, current films, both feature and documentary, can be justly criticised on this level. While writing these pages I sat through a sequence of a big film the entire story of which was told in the sound track ; I might just as well have been by my radio with my eyes shut.

Here, in passing, it should be pointed out that, despite its equal ability to reach everyone everywhere, the radio cannot claim the same creative powers as the film. In the first place, radio does not involve the gathering-together of people in groups, united by a common purpose. In the second place it has yet to prove itself an art. So far it has proved itself no more than a wonderful transmitter of another art, Music. The answer is, of course, that it is waiting for visuals. When television is fully developed the art of cinema will in essence take over the ether.

* "L'image qui ne bouge pas déconcerte l'enfant, et ce sens de mouvement, il le donne dans la gaucherie de ses dessins, comme le recherchaient les primitifs habitants de cavernes dans leurs graphites"
(*Les Grandes Missions du Cinéma*)

Making Films.

The art of film is essentially the art of manipulation of light ; photography—the reaction of a sensitized surface to light ; and composition—the making of satisfying and telling shapes out of light in movement seen within the arbitrary rectangle of the screen. Being essentially an art of two dimensions (philosophically this will remain true even of stereoscopy) it seeks constantly a third—that is, it seeks an illusion of depth and, with it, reality. Source of light, grades of light; sources of movement, direction of movement : these are the fundamentals of any given film scene. But the single scene is not the whole film; it is like a small detail from a large painting. To achieve the film proper other elements are involved.

But we must concentrate first on the visual elements of film, and observe what had been achieved without organised sound (other than a musical accompaniment) by the time the cinema was 30 years old. The revolution effected by the coming of sound was, in fact, exaggerated at the time, but it remains true that the real basis of film art had been fully established by the late 1920s, and that they depend solely on the moving *picture*.

These bases were in essence laid down by the screen's first great artist, D. W. Griffith, in a series of films made by him between 1914 and 1924, and including *Birth of a Nation, Intolerance, Way Down East, Orphans of the Storm, Broken Blossoms*, and *Isn't Life Wonderful* ? Even in a book as unhistorical as this, it is impossible to omit a tribute to the fantastic genius of this man to whom everyone in cinema, from Eisenstein to Hal Roach, owes so much.

Here are the principles discovered by Griffith and established as the unchangeable elements of cinema.

The Camera

The first principle is *the mobility of the camera*, by which the viewpoint of the audience can be constantly changed. This can be done by bringing the camera close to what is being filmed, by moving the camera about on wheels, by swinging it on cranes, and by using lenses of different focal lengths which achieve different emphases and distortions of perspective.

Thus the camera can be made to select those aspects of what is being filmed which will give the spectator the most vivid and intimate participation in the action. This mobility allows us to see a close-up of a hand nervously crumpling a handkerchief, or a vast landscape in which thousands of men surge in conflict ; it enables us to share the impressions of a locomotive engineer in a train rushing towards a broken bridge, or the slow and inevitable increase of distance between two people who are parting for ever.

For every scene in a film, therefore, the director must select that aspect, or camera angle, which best expresses mood and emotion, as well as its relation to the immediate action and to the story as a whole. This is the first creative element of the film.

Editing.

The second creative element is in cutting, editing, assembling, montage, or whatever other word you care to use to describe the fact that a film consists of strips of celluloid of varying lengths which can be joined together in varying and pre-determined lengths and order.

By doing this you can create a new sense of space and a new sense of time, both of which are peculiar to the film, in the sense that they can be achieved not by the impact of event or personality, but by means purely mechanical.

By joining various strips of film together you can relate people and things thousands of miles apart. In a film studio a man can lift up his eyes to the hills of a country the other side of the world. And, as in the crazy logic of our dreams, we may see a man decide to go to China, and, a split second later, there he is. Here the time value comes in. In the film time can be expanded or compressed at will. An action which in real life takes one minute may on the screen be expanded to ten, or contracted to a few seconds. It is interesting to test this out in a cinema by comparing what your watch says with the impression of time you are receiving from the film on the screen ; the result is always astonishing, one way or the other. Half the art of cinema consists of this sort of juggling with space and time by putting together strips of film of different content and different action.

These two principles, the position of the camera and the editing of the strips of film which it photographs, are, in essence, the bases of cinematic expression. When related to the manipulation of light, and the dynamic forms of pictorial composition within the screen frame which are peculiar to the film, they are the foundations on which everything else rests.

The Script.

In practice, however, the first job in making a film is to achieve a good script, and this, as both film-makers and their audiences so often learn to their cost, is not so easy.

Taking it by and large, the making of a film depends both on the conception and shaping of a story and on the selection of the correct visual images which, when photographed, will tell the story in the most coherent and convincing manner. The scenario and shooting script of a film, be it a love story or a sociological documentary, is a vitally important job. It is also extremely difficult, since it involves a series of acts of imagination, of seeing in the mind's eye, of guessing what the ideas and the story will look like when, at long last, they are translated into the fluid and rapidly moving medium of the screen itself. Many film-makers feel that once the script is finished at least half, or even three-quarters, of the battle is over.

The script determines what scenes are to be photographed. It determines the action which is to take place before the camera, and the angle from which that action is to be filmed. It also lays down the order of events, that is, it forecasts the basis of the editing.

But once shooting starts the other elements of the medium begin to play their part. There is the director's problem of getting the right performance out of his actors, be they professional stars or children of nature. There are a hundred and one points where the prevision of the script proves faulty ; angles are changed, action varied. And when shooting is over, the editing process raises new problems and changes, and introduces new elements not foreseen before. The making of a film is in fact as fluid as the medium itself, and if most film people seem a little mad, it is no doubt due to this essentially unpredictable quality of the medium. A film, is, indeed, as unpredictable as a dream ; but, unlike dreams, we can impose on it something of our own conscious sense of shape and purpose.

Sound.

The addition of the sound track has not altered the bases of film art, but it has extended its capabilities. The term ' silent film ' is in any case a misnomer, and has deceived a number of the younger generation, who think that before the talkie era films were projected in complete silence, broken presumably only by the sounds of striking matches, rustling paper-bags, and the sucking of hollow teeth. Yet from the earliest days of public cinema-shows a musical accompaniment was regarded as essential. It ranged from a single piano to a full symphony orchestra. Special scores were written by the hundreds, designed for all purposes, and entitled ' Enraptured Crowd,' ' Storm at Sea,' ' Mysterious Night ' and so on.* For a few films noted composers wrote carefully synchronised scores. Of these, one of the most notable was Meisel's for *The Battle Cruiser Potemkin*.

Thus film had always used sound accompaniment. The introduction of the sound track gave it the human voice. The first effect of this was disastrous. To avoid recording the noise of the camera motor all the apparatus had to be enclosed in a cumbersome sound-proof booth. The camera became static. The principles of editing were also more or less jettisoned, partly because of the cumbersome apparatus, and partly because the marvel of the 100 per cent. all-talking, all-singing super-colossal movie was considered so exciting that immense lengths of film, unvaried in angle or distance, could unroll their weary length undisturbed.

This, however, was only a passing phase. Very soon the sound-track was adjusted to meet the necessities of filmic expression, and cinema emerged enormously strengthened.

* c.f. *Film Music*, by Kurt London (v. Bibliography)

The camera became mobile again. The possibilities of editing sound were seen to be similar to those of editing visuals (after all, the sound track is a photograph too). Elaborate techniques were developed for mixing various sound tracks together, so that in the final film it is possible to present a conglomeration of sounds recorded at different places and at different times.

Moreover the creative possibilities of the sound track are considerable, once it is considered as complementary rather than supplementary to the picture. Sound can add an extra quality by saying something which is not in, but is related to, the visuals. Considerable experiment in this direction was carried out in the late twenties by the Soviet film-makers and subsequently by documentary workers in this country.

In this respect the work of the late Walter Leigh was particularly important. In one film (*Song of Ceylon*) he used all available sounds—natural effects, dialogue, songs, ' constructed ' sounds, as well as an orchestra of unusual composition—as part of a carefully worked out score, thus for the first time integrating the entire sound track into a shaped and symmetrical whole. Moreover the track had a life of its own ; and when it was allied to the picture it was clear that Leigh had achieved a new and important synthesis. The picture said one thing ; the track said something else. Together, the two produced a third quality denied to either of them separately.

A similar and only too rare approach to the sound-film is found in Carol Reed's masterpiece *Odd Man Out*. Here overtones and overlaps of sound are used with great imagination and bound in with William Alwyn's remarkable orchestral score.

Music

The role of the composer has thus become increasingly important. Composers like Leigh, Britten, Jaubert, Walton, Lambert, Milhaud, Alwyn, Bliss, Addinsell, Vaughan Williams, have turned to the sound film as a special means of musical expression, and the films of France and England have benefited accordingly. In Hollywood there has been a tendency to stereotype film music (rather as in the days of the silent film) and the skill of composers like Max Steiner and Miklos Rosza has been allowed to run'to luxuriant seed, as may be seen in such a film as *The Best Years of Our Lives*, where the unremitting lushness of the music ends by defeating legitimate dramatic ends, so that in the scene of the aeroplane junk-yard, where the music should take dramatic charge, the effect is lost through satiety.

Dialogue

Nor is there any need to minimise the value of direct synchro-nised dialogue, which has enabled good writers, to whom the screen had hitherto been closed, to exercise their dramatic and poetic skills. Shakespeare himself has reached the screen, sometimes almost unrecognisable, as in *Romeo and Juliet*, sometimes effectively, as in *Midsummer Night's Dream* and twice at least, in *Henry V*, and *Hamlet* with enormous success. Original writing for sound films has caused new techniques and tricks of expression to be developed, as they have been in the case of music.

But quite apart from all this there remains the simple fact that, in dialogue alone, the sound-film has opened up new avenues for the expression of human thought. It would never have been possible in the silent film to produce works like *The Grapes of Wrath, Dr. Ehrlich's Magic Bullet, Zola, Pasteur, Marie Walewska, Odd Man Out,* and *Paisa*. These films depend not merely on the purely visual impact, but upon the verbal expression of thoughts which in themselves are of great importance. Combined with the proper use of all the visual possibilities of the film-medium, they provide a dramatic and emotional experience of the highest order.

Such films enable a vast audience to hear and understand ideas which carry conviction because they are dramatically and aesthetically allied to the visual spectacle. Indeed, were it not for its special qualities, the cinema might be described as a new and extended form of drama. Incidentally the best textbook on film making I have ever come across is Aristotle's *Poetics* ; and I am sure Mr. Goldwyn and others would agree with him that every film ' must have six parts, which parts determine its quality—namely, Plot, Character, Diction, Thought, Spectacle, Song.'—though perhaps the fourth attribute might give one or two producers a curious feeling.

New Techniques.

The film-medium does not stand still. Soon colour will supersede monochrome films entirely, and new problems will arise in editings, and in the control and selection of colour—problems which, except possibly by Disney and McLaren have not yet been seriously tackled.

The Russians are said to have perfected the stereoscopic film, which may well prove to be the most revolutionary discovery of all. And a whole field will soon open up in the relations of the moving picture to television.

But so far I have dealt only with positive potentialities. It is now necessary to consider the equally important limitations of the medium—limitations within which all film makers must work.

It Isn't So Easy

A film is, as a rule, seen only once. You cannot easily refer back to it later on, as you can with a painting or a piece of music. All the complications of film-technique are, therefore, devoted to the production of the utmost simplicity of effect, and in this art, as in others, nothing is more complicated to achieve than the simple. It has been computed (with what accuracy I do not know) that only sixty per cent of the content of a film gets across to the average audience. But equally it is certain that the other forty per cent is essential. Attention to detail, however small, and to the slightest nuances, is the mark of every good film director. The audience may not notice them when they are there, but if they are absent the film loses much of its appeal.

The film image is flat, be it in monochrome or colour. Immense ingenuity of composition and of lighting is needed in order to achieve the illusion of depth and solidity. The direction of movement within the screen frame is, of course, t he key to the composition of a moving picture, and differen- ti ates it far more sharply from the still photograph than most people imagine. A dull movie shot is one in which the illusion of depth, and of spatial relationships in movement, has not been achieved.

Working in Groups.

To some individuals the most irksome limitation of cinema is that a film cannot be made by the efforts of one single person. The complications of the camera apparatus, of design, of lighting ; the chemical mysteries of the processing laboratories ; the problems of continuity ; all these, and many other factors, make it a matter of highly concentrated team-work. The director, in order to carry out his creative idea, needs a team of people who are not only expert in their own diverse crafts, but are also in sympathy with each other and with the director himself. If you study the credit titles of films made by the best directors you will very soon notice how the names of the same photographers, designers, assistants and editors turn up over and over again.

Thus a film is created both by the single inspiration of the director and by the collective activity and enthusiasm of a diverse group of experts who pool their skill to the agreed purpose. This sort of group activity in art may well reflect to some degree the general trends (good and bad) of Western civilisation as a whole.

Then again the individual artist—I mean Vigo, Pudovkin, Rossellini, Ford, Reed, Stroheim, Pabst, Dreyer and suchlike —has much more between his idea and its realisation than workers in other arts. A writer, painter or composer can obtain without much expense or difficulty the means of expressing his idea—pencil, paper, canvas, paint. The film-maker is not in the same position. If he writes a script, however brilliant, it does not *exist* as an artistic expression. It is not the same as the score of a symphony which *does* exist, however useless it may seem if it is never performed. The film man's idea cannot exist until it is on the screen. And between him and its realisation are all the machinery, the technicians and the costs.

Even the script of a play can be read with understanding and enjoyment, for a minor act of imagination can enable

one to picture it on the living stage. With a film script this is
just not possible ; it can give you all the detail, and it can
give you the vague overall idea, but the fluidity of the medium
itself—particularly its dependence on editing (filmic space
and time) is such that the artist's idea cannot be said to be
expressed until the actual film is finished. In this, cinema is
analogous to painting, sculpture and architecture, and, come
to think of it, the film-maker and the architect are closest
together as far as the barriers to realisation are concerned.

How Films Get Made.

Common to all the arts is the question of distribution.
The artist is a Maker. He makes things because he has something to say ; and it is a constant struggle for all artists to
get what they say transmitted to other people on a wide scale.

It may cost a novelist little more than food, drink, rent,
and some pencil and paper to express himself in a book. But
to get it circulated he has to plunge into the ramifications and
hurly-burly of the publishing and distributing trades.

The film-maker, because of the complicated technique
and the high running cost of the medium, and because of the
vast financial structure devoted to the circulation of films, is
at a special disadvantage. He is always in danger of becoming
a slave to the machine.

It has been well said that all arts exist by patronage. In
the Twentieth Century the artist has to find new patrons.
The old happy days of Popes and Princes are gone. Today
Michael Angelo would be getting his bread and butter from Shell
or I.C.I. and Sir Christopher Wren would be in the employ of
the Ministry of Works or the municipality of Atomtown.

This new patronage—the patronage of the modern state
and the modern corporation—is not necessarily a bad thing.
Like film-making itself, it reflects a logical evolution in our
technical and political organisation. Its effects are already
widely seen in posters and advertisements, in books, concerts,
recordings, and, to an increasing degree, in films.

Nevertheless, the films made directly under this sort of
patronage are still in a minority, and are mainly confined to
the documentary field—of which more will be said later.

Other than this, the creative artist finds himself in a world
of commerce, a world in which cinema has grown up lopsided,
a world in which the considerations are overwhelmingly
financial. The only exception is the Soviet Union, where the
artist works exclusively for the state. But even in that case
there can come a point where ideologies are as tyrannous as
money bags—a possibility to be remembered by all countries
which nationalise their film industries.

The Commercial Motive.

Every week, in Great Britain and the United States alone,
at least 110,000,000 million people go to the cinema. They
all pay. If the average price of a seat were as low as sixpence,
this would mean a gross receipt to the film industry of
£2,750,000 per week. Actual receipts, in this country only,
from the showing of films in public cinemas have been estimated at over £70,000,000 a year. In the United States the
film business is the third or fourth largest industry in the
country, and when you think of the U.S. output of steel and
motorcars and cotton and coal and aeroplanes, this means
something. Even in Britain the film business is now seventh
on the list of capital-employing trades.

All these visits to the cinema, all these vast sums of money,
are concerned with the film as a means of entertainment.
A film which entertains costs anything from £100,000 to
£1,000,000 to make, according to the ambition and financial
resources of the producers. Heaven knows what extra costs
are involved in the advertising and bally-hoo, and in the
building and upkeep of the movie palaces.

These facts are important. For the greatest invention since
the discovery of the printing press transmits its world-wide
message on a profit-and-loss basis almost exactly similar
to the supply of cigarettes or motor cars or refrigerators.
It is subject to the same imponderables—the unexpected
sanctions imposed not only by economic trends but also by
unpredictable variations in public taste. But, above all, it is
highly industrialised, and it is deeply involved in high finance,
both on a national and international level. Here it may be
observed that during the ' South Sea Bubble ' period of film

finance in this country (1934 to 1936), the City (notably banks, insurance companies and trusts) poured over £13,000,000 into the film industry in ten months. In 1937 the bubble burst, the banks and others got out as best they could, and the film industry collapsed, bringing with its collapse all the heartbreak of unemployment and poverty for most of its technicians.

It is just as important to understand the financial and industrial structure of the film business as it is to understand the basic principles of film art. The one is entangled in the other, and although, as we shall see later, there are other factors developing healthily outside this jungle, the fact remains that without understanding the mechanism behind the immense façade of popular movie entertainment, we cannot properly assess the realities and potentialities of the medium.

The Rise of The Tycoons.

The history of the development of the movie industry differs little from that of other new industries of modern times. The inventors did not see the commercial possibilities. Others, astute men with an acute business sense, did. Small beginnings led on to expansion. There was the inevitable period of the gold rush, followed by the equally inevitable emergence of rival interests engaged in violent internecine conflict. The weakest went to the wall, and the final and even more inevitable period of trusts and combines and integrations supervened. A few years ago it was estimated that all the vast ramifications of the United States movie industry could in the end be traced to two banking trusts—Giannini and Morgan.

So all the early romance attached to the names of Theda Bara, Thomas Ince, Mary Pickford, Douglas Fairbanks, Charlie Chaplin, de Mille, and Griffith, is completely intertwined with another set of names—Laemmle, Zukor, Loewe, Lasky, Fox, Pathé, Gaumont, Goldwyn and many others. And from the combinations of these two sets of names emerged the great trade marks of Paramount, United Artists, M.G.M., Twentieth Century Fox, R.K.O. and the rest.

In the early free-for-all days the film industry flourished equally in America and in European countries. Italy, before

World War I, produced a number of highly spectacular films ; the first film I ever saw was the Italian *Last Days of Pompeii* (1913), complete with sensational earthquake and eruption. There were also large and active industries in Britain, France, Germany and Russia.

Hollywood Takes Over.

But European production stopped during the first World War, and within those four years the American industry cornered the world market. From 1918 until very recently no serious challenge to this American domination had made itself felt. Financially and economically this fact is profoundly important, for it has made it possible for the American magnates to commit themselves to vast capital expenditure, and this in turn has enabled them to produce films of technical and spectacular quality which other countries have found it hard to beat.

This virtual monopoly by the United States has meant that the Hollywood producer has been able to count on his films making their production cost in his huge home-market, while the money coming in from overseas distribution in Europe, Asia, South America, Australasia, South Africa and the Middle East is pretty nearly sheer profit.

Conversely, the European producer has been handicapped in two ways. Firstly, his home-market is limited. Secondly, he has little or no access to the lucrative American market, nor, save on a limited scale, to markets in other parts of the world. The amount of finance available for profitable production has therefore been limited by the size of the home-market.

As I have already mentioned, the U.S.S.R. is an exception to these circumstances. The industry is state-owned, and the cinema is regarded not only as a medium of entertainment but also as a powerful educational weapon. Moreover, the potentialities of the Russian home-market are enormous.

Apart from the U.S.S.R., however, United States domination has long been a fact. The American film people are sound and acute business men, and very reasonably, have no wish to see any change in this state of affairs. Over the past twenty years they have pursued a consistent policy of buying their way into the industries of other countries. Their influence has been felt chiefly at the key-point of the industry—distribution.

The All-Powerful Middleman.

It is indeed important to realise the dominance of the distributor or renter. As middleman between the producer and the exhibitor he tends to exercise a power out of all proportion to film values. His interests are largely commercial. He has neither the creative contacts of the producer nor the appreciative (audience) contacts of the exhibitor. The fact that the cartel-like arrangements of big film business tend to put production, distribution and exhibition under the same control does not necessarily alter the key position of the renting side.

The Americans have also bought their way into production. For instance 49 per cent of the shares in the huge Associated British Pictures Corporation (founded by the late John Maxwell) are owned by Warner Brothers.

Protection.

Many attempts have been made by European countries to foster their home industries by various forms of protection. In Britain the Cinematograph Films Act of 1928 set up a quota system under which cinemas were compelled to show a percentage of British-made films—the percentage rising year by year.

The Americans countered by setting up their own production companies here, and employing British staffs to make ' quickies,' cheap and shoddy films which were often shown once only, early in the day, merely to comply with the law. The second Act of 1938 introduced a minimum required production cost in order to kill the quickie ; but in other respects it continued the same percentage system.

It is too early to know how well the new Act of 1948 will work, but it can certainly be said that it goes very much further than the previous Acts in attempting to solve the basic problems of home production. The overall cost test

will help to eliminate cheap and shoddy productions, and
the new division of film categories into Feature Films and
Supporting Films should give opportunities for new styles
of production, as well as encouraging independent film-
makers. But the confusion attendant on the Import Tax
situation and the Board of Trade's resulting deal with
Hollywood, makes it difficult to prophesy. One fact however
is clear, and that is that the situation after World War II is
considerably different from that which obtained in 1939.

The American market in Europe was cut off during the
period of Nazi domination. After liberation, there were
significant changes. Czechoslovakia, Poland and Jugoslavia
emerged with nationalised film industries. France showed
some reluctance to re-admit U.S. influence into her own
industry. Germany was in ruins.

On the other hand, there was a scarcity of films which only
Hollywood could meet. And for four or five years Europe had
seen no U.S. films, so that there was a lovely backlog of films
which had already done very nicely and which, when unloaded
onto Europe, would represent money for jam.

Both France and Czechoslovakia tried to get tough with
the U.S.A., but the scarcity factor (among others) was against
them. The final deals were, on the whole, to the advantage
of Hollywood, a fact which has engendered a good deal of
ill-feeling in the French industry.

It would, however, be unfair to regard American actions
simply as yet another example of the work of wicked financiers.
After all, the film business *is* business, and Hollywood
with its vast commitments needs to look after its markets.

One of its most vital markets, however, is Britain, which
at long last has succeeded in creating a notable production
industry of its own.

In the pre-war years the circumstances already outlined
tended to result, particularly in Britain, in unsound finance
and in violent alternations of boom and slump.

I have already mentioned the South Sea bubble period
of the thirties, in which huge sums were poured into British
films, and production costs rose to heights which were bound
to lead to a crash, since the markets were not available.

However, one concrete result did emerge from this lunatic period, and that was the building of a number of large and well equipped studios—notably Denham, Pinewood and Amalgamated (now M.G.M.). After the economic wreck these properties remained, and the productive potential of our industry was thereby increased.

Rebirth Of An Industry

Today we have a second boom period, but the circumstances are different. There has emerged the figure of Mr. Joseph Arthur Rank, the millionaire miller with a mission. It is Mr. Rank's intention to crack open the world market at all costs. As a first step he bought his way largely into all branches of the British film industry, to such an extent that in 1943 the President of the Board of Trade was moved to send for him and obtain from him a gentleman's agreement that he would curtail his activities somewhat ; in other words, the prospect of a Rank monopoly of the entire industry had reached a point at which the Government felt bound to take action. Subsequently, the Cinematograph Films Council, a somewhat shadowy body set up in 1938 by the Board of Trade, appointed, at the President's request, a Committee to investigate ' tendencies to monopoly.'

This report concluded that these tendencies did exist, and it talked learnedly of ' vertically and horizontally integrated trusts.' But no particular action was taken.

Nevertheless the controversy aroused by the emergence of Rank as the dominating figure of British films still rages. Some regard him as the one and only hope ; others claim that not only is any home monopoly a danger, having regard to the great ideological influence of the film, but also that if Rank fails the entire industry will inevitably fall under American control, thus giving Hollywood a world holding even greater than at present. Mr. Rank says blandly that he does not intend to fail ; and the argument continues.

Much of the argument involves political or sectional partisanship and various indiscriminate blasts of hot air. The sober facts are that Rank is a business man with

immense financial resources ; that he is surrounded by
lieutenants and advisers whose abilities are not always as big
as their salaries ; and that, under his aegis, British film makers
have turned out an increasing number of first class films as
well as a number of bad ones.

On the production side, such good film makers as Carol
Reed, Frank Launder, Sydney Gilliat, David Lean, Peter
Ustinov and Thorold Dickinson, have been given a greater
freedom than was ever available before, outside Sir Michael
Balcon's studio at Ealing ; and the results may be seen in
such films as *Odd Man Out, I See a Dark Stranger, School
for Secrets, Man of Two Worlds, Henry V, Hamlet* and
Great Expectations.

By committing himself to overseas distribution on a lavish
scale, Rank has begun to drive a few wedges into the American
distribution structure. So far only one film has made a real
dent in the United States home market—*The Seventh Veil*
(Sydney Box) was the first British film to impinge on American
audiences in a pretty big way from coast to coast. *Henry V*
which, like a number of other British films, has big prestige
value, is said to have made £400,000 so far ; but this has come
from special seasons at cinemas in big cities, and does not
represent wide circulation throughout the United States.
Great Expectations, on the other hand, which was the first
British film to be premiered in New York's mammoth Radio
City Music Hall, may well achieve a success at least equal
to that of *The Seventh Veil.* Meanwhile the industry has been
thrown into some confusion by the American reaction to
the Import Tax, and the resulting arrangements for a limitation on dollar earnings. In any event, there is now the
need to make less expensive films without loss of quality.

One result of the renaissance of good film-making in Britain
became very noticeable in 1946 and 1947. On all sides there
appeared fervent pro-British patriotism together with violent
attacks on the quality and content of American films. The
most odious comparisons were freely and publicly made.

Unfortunately this trend was helped by a very definite
drop in the quality of American production. With very few
exceptions the films from Hollywood followed an escapist,

shallow and often reactionary pattern, the climax of which
was seen in the ridiculous Communist-witch hunt by the so-
called Committee on Un-American Activities, which resulted
in Hollywood panic, and the dismissal of a number of first-
class film-makers. The admirable pre-war policy which
produced films like *Zola*, *Pasteur*, *Dr. Ehrlich*, *The Grapes
of Wrath*, and *The Oxbow Incident* seemed to have been
abandoned, with a few rare exceptions like *Boomerang* and
(within its self-imposed limits) *The Best Years of our Lives*.

But the fostering by British film critics of a rather humour-
less anti-American campaign can hardly be described as
sensible tactics. Much of the product of any film industry
anywhere is pretty poor. If you go to France and see the sort of
film which doesn't get exported for showing in our specialised
cinemas here, you receive a depressing eyeful. And so far
as Britain is concerned we can hardly be proud of our Wicked
Ladies, Magic Bows, Hungry Hills, and Idols of Paris.

The inescapable fact is that the structure and commitments
of the entertainment film industry impose a level of, shall
we say ? mediocre competence on some 80% of its output,
and that is true of any country.

The Vicious Circle.

The cinemas provide mass entertainment on a scale never
before imagined. What that entertainment is like is largely
determined by the distribution and exhibition side of the
business. Theoretically speaking, if people don't like a film
it doesn't make money from its exhibition, and the producers
don't make any more films like that. Conversely, if audiences
like a film, it does make money and the producers make more
of the same sort. In actual practice, however, the industry
has become so huge, and audiences have become so conditioned to going to movies, that any given bad film is not
necessarily a financial failure. People go to the cinema any-
way, and if this week's film is not so good as last week's they
seldom remove their custom or complain to the manager.

Hence has arisen what appears to be a vicious circle. The
film people say they give the public what it wants, and the

public, by habit, takes what it is given. Over a period, however, the trend of public reaction may have a definite effect on the trade. For instance, people everywhere began to desert the cinemas during the mid-twenties. Stage shows and orchestras and music-hall turns were introduced to bolster up the failing films, but to no avail. It was at this point that the talking film, whose apparatus had long been available, was introduced, and the situation was, by a novelty, saved. Similarly there comes a point when, in a vague way, audiences appear to be sated by a particular type of film, and thereupon the gangster or war-film cycle comes to an end and another cycle, maybe sophisticated comedy or fake psychiatry, begins. The present period of retrenchment in Hollywood is due to an alarming drop in box-office receipts during 1947, a drop which occurred not only overseas, but also in the U.S. market itself.

Ballyhoo.

Another thing which the average movie-goer does not realise is how far his movements are influenced by the carefully calculated flow of publicity. He may think he has complete freewill as to what film he goes to see, but in point of fact the reason he finds himself in the Bijou seeing *Slap it Again* is in great measure due to the skill with which the advance publicity has seeped in on him ' constantly, painlessly, obliquely, without his really being aware of its presence until the moment for action comes '—to quote from Margaret Thorp's admirable book *America at the Movies*. I sometimes wish that more members of the public would read occasionally a few issues of the trade press of the film industry—admirable and readable journals, with a style peculiarly their own. In these papers—*The Kinematograph Weekly* and *Today's Cinema*, in this country, *Variety* and *Motion Picture Herald* in America —they would find an approach and attitude to films which would perhaps surprise and would certainly enlighten them.

The diehards of the film trade, who are the first to claim that cinema is an art when someone attacks them on its being an industry, and with equal passion claim it is an industry when someone tries to market an unusual, artistic, or out-of-the-rut film, will hotly deny the substance of the preceding

few paragraphs, and with hand on heart will claim that they
are no more than the servants of the cinema-going public.
This attitude does them and their business a disservice.

Problems of the Box-office.

In common with most normal people I have a great liking
for and admiration of the movie-business. I go to the cinema
whenever I get the chance, and I like all sorts of films. But,
again like most movie-goers, I sometimes sigh for something
better or different, and it is no good the trade trying to smother
the sighs (or the yawns) with protestations that it's my fault.

On the other hand, it's no joke to make films for a world
market. Your audience consists of all sorts of people—
farmers, housewives, children, sophisticates, illiterates, slum-
dwellers, capitalists, professors, stevedores, Europeans,
Asiatics, Africans, Cabinet Ministers, convicts, generals,
students, lowbrows, highbrows, film-stars and film-technicians.
How are you to please the greatest number, having regard
to the prime fact that unless they pay to see your films you go
bankrupt, and that the regular costs of production, distribution, exploitation and exhibition are astronomical ?

The first and easiest answer, which indeed set the pace
for the industry in its surging pioneer days, is to go for the
Lowest Common Denominator. You look around the great
wide world, and you see that the vast majority of people
have not enough money or food or work, that they have not
enough happiness and can see little save dreams over the
horizon, and that they are not very well educated. You make
films for this vast majority. And you provide pipe dreams
and wish fulfilments and anything which takes people away
from the hard realities of life. You find that people like
what you give them, and ask for more. You give it them,
and the vicious circle begins.

There is little doubt that the bad reputation of the cinema,
which still persists today, particularly among magistrates
who attribute all juvenile delinquency to the influence of the
films (how easy and comforting not to probe into the real
reasons, which are much more disturbing), rests on the fact

that in the early days films were made, on the whole, for the 'lower classes.' Those were the days when the flicks were for the housemaids ; genteel people went to the theatre.

The Virtuous Circle.

What is more important to note is that on both sides—audience and film production—standards have been steadily rising for the past twenty years. There appears to be a virtuous as well as a vicious circle. There is little doubt that today the yearly percentage of good films is considerably greater than it was even ten years ago. To assess all the reasons is difficult. But it seems pretty obvious that on the one hand the industry is attracting creative workers of higher and higher quality (the introduction of sound has probably had a lot to do with that) and on the other the public is becoming more and more discriminating in its choice of films—despite the ballyhoo. There are even signs, faint though they may be, of a raising of standards in the film criticisms in the daily press. But whatever the reasons, the movie-business is not standing still ; it is well to remember that out of the morass of indifferent rubbish of the past quarter century there has appeared more than a handful of real masterpieces, and several bushels of first class, honest, useful films.

Today, with the shake-up of values administered by World War II, with the new awareness and assessment of facts and fancies in the minds of ordinary people everywhere, the film industry is faced with the challenge of taking the lead in improving the quality of its product, and not, as sometimes in the past, lagging reluctantly behind.

What We Want.

In other words we are not concerned with whether or no the wicked American magnates are becoming deeply perturbed at the threat of the British film to dollar imperialism. We are concerned with what all film makers everywhere can do in terms of the new emphases and realities of the world today.

This does not mean taking up a highbrow attitude and demanding that every film shall be a masterpiece ; one might as well expect a Picasso on every chocolate box. One can, however, demand that films should at least be well, not shoddily made, that they should tell their story with imagination and in conformity with a reasonable level of good taste, and above all that their story should be a good one, chosen carefully for its particular purpose, even if that purpose be no more that to give us a good laugh (and what could be better than that ?)

We have come to a point in history when consideration of real needs rather than of impossible fantasies is the only true yardstick. It is the point at which the role of the film must be subjected to new and rigorous judgment, not just by idealists and reformers, but by the very people who still control the bulk of the film-output of the world—commercial film producers, distributors, and exhibitors.

Meantime the other possibilities of the film medium are beginning to mature and make themselves felt, and it is necessary to consider how far they have already developed and what promise they hold for the future.

II. FANTASY AND FACT.

THE cinema was not invented with the purpose of money-making in mind. The research and experiment which led to the development of cinematography was carried out by scientists who were seeking to analyse motion. Thus the biologist Marey, in 1880, developed an apparatus which he called the ' Chronophotograph.' This enabled him to record movements which hitherto had not been observed owing to the fact that they were too fast to match man's abilities of visual perception. Marey went no further than this, and it was left to Edison, Friese-Greene and the Lumières to perfect the actual film apparatus. Neither realised its potentialities, and Edison in particular did not at first even bother to patent his discovery; in his grand way he seems to have invented for the sake of inventing.

But once it was invented, many scientists quickly realised the importance of the film to their work. As early as 1899 Dr. Doyen, in France, was recording his own surgical technique on film ; and by 1909 Commandon, also in France, was projecting films of microbes to the Academy of Sciences. Commandon is still at work today, at the head of groups of scientists of whom de Fonbrune, with his wonderful micro-forge and micro-manipulator, is the most noted.

In the same early days the film medium was seized on by a French conjuror and illusionist, Georges Melies. He realised its enormous possibilities as far as his own work was concerned, and proceeded to make a great number of film fantasies which are still notable for exuberance of imagination and an extraordinary prophetic use of all sorts of film-tricks and devices. Such films as *A Trip to the Moon* and *Voyage à travers l'Impossible* represent a use of the medium which has since been more or less neglected except by such cartoonists as Harriman, of Krazy Kat fame, and by Disney in his earlier and better days. Melies work was soon forgotten, and he died in poverty a few years before World War II. His funeral, unlike his declining years, was honoured by noted figures

from the film industry ; but film makers, with the exception
of Cavalcanti, have not remembered and understood the
nonsense-verse quality of Melies work.

Thus the early days of cinema were the days of the scientist
and the fantasist. The photography of stage-plays, and the
development of the novelette film, came later. But, as we have
seen, when it came it swamped everything.

Beyond The Box-Office.

But all along the brilliant rocket-trail of the entertainment
film there have been pale, almost unnoticed glimmers.
Throughout the 50 years of cinema's history small groups
and individuals, usually working under severe limitations
of equipment and finance, have pursued paths outside the
world of entertainment.

In France and pre-Hitler Germany, Britain, Holland,
Belgium and the U.S.A., the Avant Garde made experiments
in abstract films, surrealist films, trick films, hand-drawn
films and other approaches to cinematic expression which
were outside the general run of box-office.

Scientists and educationists in many countries did likewise
in their own fields. In this country there were, for instance,
Dr. Canti's micro-studies of cancer-growths, and Percy
Smith's remarkable film records of biological processes of
all kinds, to which he devoted 37 years of constant experiment.
Smith's partnership with Bruce Woolfe in the *Secrets of Nature*
(later *Secrets of Life*) series was for many years Britain's
sole claim to recognition as a producer of worth-while films.

Films for both school and agricultural education were used
fairly regularly in France from 1916, in Germany from 1918
and Japan from 1920 onwards. The U.S.S.R. entered this
field on a very large scale immediately the State took over
the entire film industry in 1919. In the U.S.A. Eastman Kodak
sponsored a report by Professors Wood and Freeman on
Motion Pictures in the Classroom, and built up an extensive
library of educational films. Later, the Western Electric
Corporation took similar action through its subsidiary,
Electrical Research Products Inc. (E.R.P.I.), which produced
and distributed a large number of educational films.

In this field Britain lagged far behind, and as late as 1932 the Commission on Education and Cultural Films was able, without much exaggeration, to state that ' Cinematography in Great Britain has endured the neglect and scorn of those who control the education of the young. For many years most teachers and administrators ignored films. Those who thought about them ... were concerned almost exclusively with attempts to restrict the attendance of children at public cinemas.'

Problems of Patronage.

In general it can be said that these two streams of experimental effort—one concerned with developing the expressive powers of cinema, and the other with its value to science and instruction—were for years handicapped by lack of money, apparatus, and markets. For the structure of the film industry itself, being based largely on the profit motive, provides little or no opportunity for the avant-gardist or the educationist. For both, therefore, the problem of patronage or sponsorship is the main problem.

In general it is less difficult to obtain sponsorship for technical or education films than for experiments in film aesthetic, since for the former there is an organised and functional role in terms of community or state needs.

Subsidy on the educational levels can come from two main sources. At one end of the scale is whole-scale State-ownership of production and distribution, as in the U.S.S.R. At the other is the self-interest of manufacturers like that of Kodak and E.R.P.I. to which I have already referred. Both of these sponsors were of course motivated by self-interest, since they manufacture film and film apparatus. But in these cases motive is less significant than results.

Films Are Expensive.

It is a fallacy to suppose that a film for teaching or instructional purposes, however simple those purposes may be, is cheap to make. It is one thing for a research worker to make his own amateur film for his own records purposes ; bad photography, scratched film and other faults make not much difference to him in his laboratory. But a film which is to have wide circulation in classrooms and colleges must not merely have the highest ' production value ' (comparable in degree to that of a Hollywood film) but must also be based on the most expert knowledge and must be so laid out as to explain its subject matter in the clearest possible way. This involves research, experiment and time ; and these cost plenty.

When the films have finally been made the cost of producing them may have to be recouped, as in the entertainment world, from the audiences. But projection apparatus is also costly, and education authorities and schools often can't afford to instal it. Or if they can, they can't, in addition, afford the rentals which the producing company has to charge in order to ensure covering its production cost, and a bit over.

Technical Problems.

The second main obstacle lies in the fact that films are not only expensive, but also technically complicated and difficult to make. The teacher has no time to master the art and skill of film-making. The film-maker cannot become expert in the equally complicated and difficult art of teaching. The same situation applies to the realm of the scientific and technological film.

The sort of movies required must therefore be the result of a close collaboration between the film makers on the one hand and the teachers, scientists, and technicians on the other. And unfortunately this is where, hitherto, the whole scheme has broken down. Teachers enthusiastic over the use of films have had their ardour dampened by the discovery that the films at their disposal are often ill-designed for their purpose, or are merely travelogues masquerading as teaching films. The film producers, on the other hand, have found themselves working in the dark, since they have had no authoritative central body to consult on the type and style of their films. When sections or individuals in the teaching profession have been consulted, their opinions have been vague, conflicting and usually contradictory.

It has been equally difficult, and for similar reasons, to achieve proper co-operation between the film-maker and the scientist or technologist.

Where The Money Comes From.

To ensure the organised development of both aesthetic and instructional work in films, sources of finance have to be sought outside the film industry itself. In this Britain has provided the most successful solution so far in the form of the documentary movement, which, since 1928, when John Grierson started work on *Drifters*, has made notable contributions to the film both as an art form and as an educational force.

Much has already been written on documentary*, and it would be absurd on my part to repeat what has already been well said. But the documentary theory propounded and put into practice by Grierson and his colleagues has had such far-reaching effects that it is necessary to examine its purpose and significance in some detail, if we are to get a clear idea of future developments in the world of film.

The Bases of Documentary.

The documentary method is in fact *a method of approach to public enlightenment, information and education.* It is not confined to the film medium, but is concerned too in all the new media of mass-communication—press, radio, television, exhibitions and the rest. It has been successful because it is based on certain needs and problems which are a definite part of the modern state, and of the relations between one state and another.

By the 1920's it had become clear that Western democracy was in danger of collapse because its citizens did not know how to make it work. Life, the machinery of life, had become so complex that the average man found himself ill-adapted to understand the issues of the day and, more importantly, his own position and responsibility in relation to those issues. The economic system of the great Victorian era was falling apart. The political system was in danger of complete collapse, not so much through threats of revolution as through electoral apathy. People had become bewildered because life had begun to move too fast for them.

This basic failure in democracy was a failure in education.

* *Grierson on Documentary,* edited by Forsyth Hardy, *Documentary Film* by Paul Rotha, and *The Factual Film,* an Arts Enquiry Report (see Bibliography).

Pedagogics Are Not Enough.

Heaven knows there was education of a sort for nearly everyone. But it was limited, unimaginative. It was devoted to facts, to knowledge for the sake of knowledge. It gave nothing related to people's everyday lives and problems. In a complex technological world the ordinary man found himself without any proper bearings ; and official education gave him virtually no help.

Education in its true sense—its relation to life—had really passed into the hands of people who were not educationists at all—the people who ran the newspapers, magazines, advertising (including in U.S.A. the radio), and the cinema. Because these people have had to consider—if only superficially—the real needs and instincts of people ; because they have had to use dramatic and exciting methods (otherwise where would the profits be ?), they have provided valuations which definitely arise from observing man's daily experiences in a difficult and complicated world.

The standards were no doubt low. But the fact remained—and remains—that ordinary people are no fools. In the complexity of the modern world they may not be able to know everything about everything all the time, but, as John Grierson puts it, ' they have an unerring sense of smell.' If films and newspapers and radio create loyalties where educators do not, then it is high time for the educators to do something positive about it.

The basis of the documentary method, as propounded and developed by Grierson, was to use those very phenomena of the complex machine age—the new systems of mass entertainment which were annihilating space and bringing the same ideas and standards (not always very high ones) to millions of people all over the world—to use them for education in the widest and most imaginative sense of the word.

Film was chosen, rather than any other medium, because the gift of sight is common to all men. Seeing is believing. Sight knows no language barriers ; and, as I have already pointed out, the moving-picture has a particular and deep-rooted appeal. It is vivid, easy to understand, and convincing.

Meeting a Need.

Documentary succeeded because it was designed to meet the needs and problems I have just indicated. It offered a solution to a problem which affected everyone, and therefore *it found finance.* Not finance from the big film companies, but from Government departments and from the public relations officers of big public utility corporations.

By interpreting to men their relation to society, by presenting everyday life in its exciting aspects ; and by giving people a sense of dignity and of shared problems and responsibilities, the documentary film rapidly took its place as a key factor in the field of public information and public enlightenment. Its method,—the documentary method— was soon adopted in other media. Today you have the documentary broadcasts, documentary pamphlets, even documentary novels.

What Documentary Does.

The documentary film itself has been defined as a film which is a creative interpretation of reality. A true documentary must have imaginative drive, original techniques, in a word, the creative spark. In this strict sense the development of the documentary movement has played some part in solving the problem of the avant garde as well as of the educationist. Documentary has always been noted for bold experiment. Not a few of its films have been widely acclaimed as works of art. Under its banner original and unique artists like Len Lye and Norman McLaren have found finance and facilities denied to them elsewhere.

On the other side of the picture, the documentary method, as opposed to the documentary film proper, has revolutionised the structure and organisation of public information on a mass scale. Within the orbit of the documentary system come all sorts of technical and instructional films, and such new developments as visual units.

Visual units consist in essence of a battery of visual material grouped round a central focus point which is a film. Thus an educational film like *Instruments of the Orchestra*, which provides a living and imaginative description of how an orchestra works, has added to it film strips, still photographs and diagrams, teachers notes and other printed and illustrated material, and, quite possibly, a travelling exhibit which can be set up in a school hall. All the visual means of education are in fact properly integrated.

New Audiences.

Documentary has had more than a little influence on current methods and conceptions of public enlightenment. It has brought new possibilities and offered new solutions to the problems which were stated at the beginning of this chapter—the problems of providing proper opportunities to those who are trying to develop new paths in cinema.

Today there is a vast public which sees films in places other than the cinemas. It was Grierson who pointed out, at an early stage in the development of documentary, that there are more seats outside the cinemas than in them. He meant the chairs and benches of schools, colleges, lecture rooms, town and village halls, and all the places where people gather together for social meetings, for discussion, or for learning.

This new audience consists to a large extent of the people who go to public cinemas. But they are in a different mood— a mood of interest, inquisitiveness, active enquiry and discussion, rather than in a mood for relaxation or vicarious entertainment.

In the British Isles this new audience for non-theatrical shows numbers nearly 20 million annually. Proportionately large audiences exist in Canada, the U.S.A., and U.S.S.R.; and there are growing audiences in most other countries where films are made or used.

The Box-office of Ideas.

The production and distribution of films for these audiences works to a pattern entirely different from that of the commercial world. The cost of making a film is not expected to be re-couped from its distribution. On the contrary, most non-theatrical distribution is provided free. Its direct cost to the audience is no greater than the cost of mailing the copies of the films back to the distribution centre. Non-theatrical film shows tend, therefore, to be a community service.

Equally the makers of the films are not speculating with their own (or other people's) money in the hopes of getting back their production cost, plus a profit, from the non-theatrical audience. Those who have tried to make films of educational or informational value in terms of the commercial film-market have nearly always fallen flat. The odds, under the present system, are too heavily against them.

In the first place, to make a short documentary film lasting 20 minutes is likely to cost over £5,000. Obviously this amount of money can only be re-couped, if at all, from the public cinemas.

In order to get the film into the cinemas, it must be made to conform to certain arbitrary standards of box-office, standards which are both conservative and shallow. The content of the film suffers accordingly.

Worse still ; even if the film is box office, its share of the money paid in to the cinemas by you and me, the audience, is minimal. It has been calculated that under the system of showing two feature films in each programme, the receipts are allocated in the ratio of as much as 95% for the features, leaving 5% to be divided between the newsreels and the rest of the supporting programme—which is where you will find your documentary.

It is therefore a stroke of luck if, over a period of two years, a short documentary nets as much as £2,000. A loss of £3,000 per film is hardly a practical proposition.

Legislation by governments, or a new policy on the part of the film industry, or both, will be necessary before this state of affairs can be remedied. Meantime, the only documentaries which can get into the public cinemas are those made on the same system as for non-theatrical distribution—that is, under a system in which the return of the entire cost of production is not expected.

The only exceptions are documentaries which are in effect feature films. If their treatment is skilful enough, and if they meet the rather vague requirements of box office, they may make money. Films which have done this include

Target for Tonight, *Western Approaches*, and *Children on Trial*. All these were made with Government money, and not speculatively. Such films are rare, and there have been a number of other documentary features which, not always through intrinsic faults of their own, have been failures at the box office.

Whatever the rights and wrongs of the case may be—and personally I think it is quite wrong that good documentaries, of any length, should be denied adequate showing in cinemas—it is clear that if the film is to play a part, and it should be a big one, in education and public enlightenment, the development of a free distribution service becomes inevitable.

Films as a Public Service.

Non-profit finance for the making and showing of documentary films is available because, in the modern state, a service of public information and education is a necessary and integral part of government and administration. There are still some who oppose this idea because they fear the misuse of film and radio by the party in power—and they quote the perversion of Germany by the late Dr. Goebbels and his henchmen. All they are really saying is that anything can be used for bad purposes as well as good. In fact, the positive need is stronger than the negative danger.

It is a fact that without an informed public the democratic process no longer works. It is necessary for the Government to explain the reasons for its actions to the people who voted it in, and to relate those reasons to the wider scene. It is necessary to explain the machinery and function of administration, both local and central, to the only people who can make it work—the ordinary citizens themselves.

By the same token the fullest use of the media like film and radio must not be denied to the educational system. And as, in this country at any rate, education is already a function of the state, there is a clear argument for films and radio programmes to be included in the system as, to a limited degree, they already are.

In any case the development of information services, including very particularly films, was forced on the Government during the war*. We now have extensive machinery for Government film making, although this does not necessarliy mean we are using it to full effect.

New Patrons.

A further development, unique to this country, has been the entry of public utility and manufacturing concerns into the information field. This arose from the adoption of public relations in addition to direct advertising. The bigger concerns realised some time ago that they were losing touch with their customers, and that their customers were in turn beginning to get awkward ideas about them. The public in fact was beginning to think of one concern as old-fashioned, another as a money-grabber, another perhaps as a plain racket.

There was a need in fact for the providers to enter into new relations with the consumers. Certain far-sighted public relations officers realised that they could equate their own local needs to the wider needs of the community. Thus you had the Gas interests making important and widely noted films on sociological problems such as slums, nutrition, education, smoke abatement and local government. In so doing they were providing a community service and at the same time they transformed their relations with the public from negative to positive. Nor did it escape their notice that new housing, new schools, better food and cooking, and fewer open coal fires would mean more business for Gas. In this sense, therefore, the purely commercial aspect became closely related to public service. Many other big corporations took similar action. Of these by far the most notable has been Shell, which has set up virtually a world-wide distribution system of first-class technical and instructional films produced largely by its own unit.

It is indeed curious to note that these forward-looking films have been made mainly by big capitalist organisations, and that until quite recently the powerful left-wing bodies such as the Unions and the Co-operatives have been extremely backward and unimaginative in their approach to films.

* For a description of this important development see *The Factual Film*, Chapter II.

Their attitude has been, with few exceptions, narrowly parochial or naively propagandist. With funds and organisation fully available for the making of inspiring films which would be of direct service to the community, they have tended to spend their money on movies devoted to celebrating centenaries and past triumphs, or to preaching to the converted. Today wiser counsels are beginning to prevail.

All Sorts and Conditions.

Any analysis of the audience for non-theatrical films reveals a remarkable cross-section of the community. You will find medical students seeing on the screen details unavailable to them from their fixed and distant position in the operating theatre ; parents seeing films about the care of their children's eyes, ears, teeth, and about their psychological relations; women's institutes seeing films not only on cooking, nutrition or household hints, but also on world-wide problems as well as aspects of local government affecting them in parish, district or county ; farmers, farm-workers, and young farmers clubs studying, through film, new techniques, new machines, new methods of controlling disease in livestock and pests of trees and plants, and, just as importantly, the relation of British agriculture to world problems of production and supply ; conferences of engineers or explorers or stamp-collectors using films for exchange of information and discussion ; soldiers, sailors and airmen learning from film the operation of intricate tank or gun or plane mechanism, or the wider aspects of tactics and strategy ; biologists, chemists, physicists, scientists and research workers in all fields studying in film not merely new techniques or theories, but also the relations of scientific and technological developments to the general structure of modern society ; members of film societies grouped together to study the history of cinema in its aesthetic and sociological aspects ; school children, students and teachers finding in films a new extension of the blackboard and the map, finding too that films are opening the classroom windows onto the wider world outside, a world of which they are already a part and into which they must soon fully enter. These are only a few examples of the new and vital audiences being reached by film.

Of these there are three groups which deserve detailed consideration—the film societies, the scientists, and the school children.

Film Societies.

Film societies exist in most countries. In many they are comparatively powerful and well-organised groups, financed by members subscriptions and holding regular shows at which films of historical, artistic, social, or experimental interest are shown. They fulfil an important function in terms of film appreciation, for they give people the opportunity to study the best, or even the unusual, in film production, and thereby help them to develop higher standards of criticism about the films which they see in the ordinary cinema from week to week. They also provide a much needed historical perspective. For with film, unlike books, reference back is difficult for the individual. It is only through film societies that people can study, say, the films of Melies in the same way as the art student can, from the book or gallery, study primitive Italian art.

Unfortunately, it was only late in the day that there arose any organised preservation of films, such as is now undertaken by the Museum of Modern Art Film Library in New York, the National Film Library in London, and the Cinemathèque Francaise in Paris. Many films of merit and interest have been lost for ever. That so many others have been unearthed, or saved from destruction by owners who saw no further monetary use for them, is due in no small measure to the drive and vigour of the film society movement. Another example of this vigour is to be seen in the International Festival of Documentary Films organised by the Edinburgh Film Guild, one of the most progressive and successful of all film societies. This festival looks like becoming an annual event.

Science Stakes a Claim.

One of the more striking developments of the past few years has been the rise of the Scientific Film Societies. This is a phenomenon particular to Britain, though our example is now being copied elsewhere, notably in Canada. It was just before the war that a small group formed the first scientific film society in London. Its object was to provide regular showings of films drawn from the widest scientific fields all over the world—not only highly technical and specialised films, but also films about the use or misuse of science in the world today.

Right from the start the members consisted both of scientists and specialists and of interested laymen. Thus not only on the screen, but also in the cinema or hall, the scientific and lay world were satisfactorily intermingled.

Within a very short time scientific film societies, big and small, sprang up with great rapidity all over the place, despite the inevitable difficulties and dislocations caused by the war. The vivid universal language of the screen attracted these men and women who were trying to bring science out of its ivory tower into the hurly burly of *realpolitik* and the hard facts of a world gone mad.

So great was the demand that within a few years there was formed a national organisation covering all scientific film activities. This body, known as the Scientific Film Association, represents the interests of film users on a very wide scale. Its influence and activity are not only national, but international as well, as is evidenced by the International Scientific Film Congress held in Paris in October 1947, which was organised by the SFS in collaboration with the French, and by the subsequent congress held in London in 1948.

Children and Teachers.

In the schools of this country the picture is less rosy. For many years the Board of Education evinced a passionate lack of interest in the film as an educational medium, and it was not until the end of the thirties that, in its *Handbook of Suggestions for Teachers*, it gave them its official blessing.

Today the Ministry of Education, risen phoenix-like from the Board, is following a more progressive course. It is deeply committed to the making and use of films for schools, and has set up two Committees to plan films and visual units and to ensure that teachers, inspectors, local administrators and (not least) film makers and other experts are brought together for discussion and action on a practical level.

But the hard fact remains that in the 30,000 schools in England and Wales there are only 1,700 film projectors— and of these 1,300 cannot project sound films. Nor are the projectors of standard size ; and a number are obsolete or obsolescent. These figures show that in comparison with North America and many European countries, England is in the Dark Ages.

Under present circumstances it will be some years before every school can have, as it should, at least one sound projector and several film-strip projectors. So far there have been no standard specifications and no date-lines laid down. Without these, manufacturers cannot be expected to go in for projector-making on a big scale, or at a price which will be sufficiently economical for the purses of Local Education Authorities (even though a 50% grant from the Ministry is available to authorities installing projectors in their schools, the present cost of at least £150 makes it too expensive for many).

Meantime the films which are being made for school use will have a circulation severely limited by projector supply. The use of shared mobile projectors, travelling from school to school, may be of temporary assistance, but this system is not satisfactory, since the visit of the projector can seldom be geared properly to the curriculum or to other school activities.

Of course, much experimental work has to be done in the making of teaching films, and the results of these experiments have to be tested in use. This can be done even during this period of projector-deficiency, but it is urgently necessary to put supply operations into action as soon as possible. Otherwise we shall be making educational films which only a very small percentage of our school children will ever see !

These gloomy prognostications must not, however, be allowed to overshadow the total world strength of the film outside the cinemas. In schools this country may be behind-hand; in other aspects of film we are pioneers.

In North America films in schools are used on a wide scale,

though there appears to be some lack of imagination both in their making and their use. But the purchase of the E.R.P.I. film library by the University of Chicago through Encyclopaedia Britannica Films Inc. is an important event, and may lead to many new developments.

New Films Mean New Methods.

As we have seen, a whole new film production system has arisen to meet the needs of the new audiences. Film companies and film units now specialise in the production of educational, instructional and documentary films, as well as in the planning of visual units and the preparation of film-strips.

While the actual mechanism, that is the camera, recording apparatus, and editing equipment, does·not differ as between feature and documentary film-production (though the latter tends to use it on a more modest scale), the technique and the thought-processes involved are very different. The growth of the use of films as a public service has very properly brought into being a large group of film-makers who are in no way interested in the bright lights, ballyhoo, and financial splendours and miseries of the entertainment film business. More and more it has come to be realised that special training and special aptitudes are needed for the documentary approach.

More and more too the film makers in this field are thinking of their films not as single entities but also as series. For it is hardly possible, in terms of discussion or even of plain information, to deal with a typical subject, for example child-parent relations, in one single film. It is necessary to plan six or even a dozen films on a subject, and the whole project therefore involves a long-term scheme. Similarly, the films must be worked out in close conjunction with the other media.

Today a documentary worker, faced with a problem, must assess the respective values of the various media, and apportion his efforts accordingly. Sometimes he may reject the film medium altogether, and hand the problem to other colleagues. More often he will, after study, decide on what film, or group of films, are required—that is, what angles of approach and

statement over what period and to what audience groups.
He will combine with workers in other media at the earliest
possible stage, so that the fullest planning may be achieved
when the situation is still fluid enough to allow of alterations
in detail and the discovery of new growing points.
Thus in documentary it is not only the making of films
which is (inevitably) a group activity. The whole process is
a group activity of all the related visual media. Truism though
this may be, it still needs stressing, if only because only group
effort can satisfactorily solve group problems. We are dealing
with groups, not individuals. The individual is interesting
because he is part of a group. His relation to the group—
his aspirations, achievements, participation or lack of it ;
his function as a unit with free-will working in consideration
of a group-unit with a group-will—all this makes the individual
more moving, thrilling, real and valuable than any conception
of him as a solitary, golden creature of nature, which to an
increasing degree he most certainly is not.

The Amateur.

So far we have dealt with professional film makers. The
Amateur also has a potentially important place in the world
of non-theatrical film. Despite the technical limitations
which have already been referred to, there is much that the
amateur can do, provided that he keeps within his own limits
and does not, as has happened only too often in the past,
attempt to emulate the drawingroom comedies or the thrillers
of the professional cinema.

What the amateur can do is to use his camera and his
editing bench to record the activities and problems which
occur in his own milieu, both in terms of his community-group
and in terms of his own job and interests.

In this connection an article by Arthur Elton in *Documentary News Letter* some three years ago is of significance. He points out that eventually the mass production
of 16mm. film cameras and projectors will mean a drop in
their prices so that ' everyone who can afford a portable
typewriter will also be able to afford a film camera. The film-
camera and film projector will become as necessary as the

typewriter, the fountain pen and the watch,' Elton goes on
to point out that in these terms it will be possible for the non-
professional film-makers to produce filmic equivalents of
' the parish magazines, learned periodicals, local papers,
minority pamphlets, and all the other commonplaces of
literature and free speech.' He goes on to point out that just
as at least a certain standard of literacy is essential for writing
even a parish magazine article, so, if the powers of film are
not to be wasted, ordinary people must know as much film-
grammar as they know written grammar as a form of expressing their thoughts. ' It will be necessary ' he concludes
' to add instruction on film-making to the curricula of our
schools, and to open classes in film making for adults.'

There is no doubt that there will be a great field for local
and parochial endeavour as the apparatus for amateur films
becomes more and more easily available. Such work will
supplement the activities of the professionals, and will cover
many aspects of individual effort and local activity which
it will be beyond the powers of the professionals to deal with.

Will Hollywood Cash In ?

So far, in considering the way films can be used outside
the entertainment film industry, I have emphasised two
factors—the patronage or sponsorship of ·production for
purposes other than immediate profit from the films themselves, and the tendency for distribution to be organised on
a non-paying basis as a community service. With certain
exceptions this is a true picture of the system up to the present.
But there are signs of change—and some of them raise
disturbing questions.

It is perhaps inevitable that the film trade itself, having
scorned and neglected the non-theatrical film for many years,
should now be beginning to sit up and take notice. For if
largely without its support, and often in spite of its opposition*,
a quite significant branch of film production and film-use has
come into existence, there may well be money in it.

* It was for a long time claimed that non-theatrical distribution was
a direct threat to box-office business, and many efforts were made to
try and put strict limits to its scope. Even today less farsighted film
people raise a howl from time to time.

Today the big Hollywood firms, and particularly Metro Goldwyn Mayer, are already beyond the planning stage in a vast scheme to corner the world non-theatrical market. Details are not fully available, but it is known that there are schemes for mobile prefabricated cinemas which will travel about in countries where regular cinemas are few and far between and will give shows *of entertainment films* on a paying basis. Other schemes involve the idea of tied projectors— that is, the company will provide a permanent projector or the regular visit of a projector to a community (a village for instance) on the understanding that regular showings of the company's film productions are given—again on a paying basis.

It is likely, of course, that such a scheme would be of great social benefit if the community is also free to use the projector for any other purpose it wishes. It is equally possible that severe restrictive practices might be indulged in by the projector suppliers in the course of cut-throat competition with their rivals. This would in the end depend on the imagination, forethought and social conscience of the film industrialists.

There is, however, a risk that, superimposed on the present system of free showings, there may be a complete system of non-theatrical entertainment film distribution. This would in effect make the market outside the cinemas the same as the present market inside the cinemas, with the result that films of information and enlightenment would be at a disadvantage.

Present indications are that the first developments would be in countries where cinemas are few and far between. It is significant that the big film companies are showing special interest in the Near and Middle East, and that they have from time to time been at some pains to re-assure cinema-owners in the United States that they have no fear of untoward competition at home.

The capital investment involved in setting up this sort of distribution in the Middle and Far East, and in Africa, would be very considerable. Whatever their motives or policy, the film-magnates would in effect be providing a wonderful extension of the power of the film medium of which govern-

ments and others would be able to make use, even if it meant
entering the field in a commercial and competitive sense.

Moreover, it is very unlikely that commercial producers
would speculate in the more specialised types of film. The cost
of making a series of films on medical or surgical techniques,
for instance, would still be out of proportion to the receipts
coming in from the audiences, which would naturally be comparatively small (hospitals, medical faculties, training centres)
and would certainly not be able to pay inflated prices for
the films.

The Best of Both Worlds.

Either, then, the valuable and growing use of specialised
films will be frozen to death by neglect, or there will have to
be a double system under which free distribution will be
carried out, as now,. on a sponsored basis, for specialised
films, while all other types will be involved in a purely commercial market. There is, of course, the other possibility that
some countries may by legislation retain control of the whole
non-theatrical field.

It is important not to overstress the possible conflict
between commercial films and sponsored films. Taking
organised education as an example, there is no doubt that
there will be financially sound possibilities for film-production
once there are projectors and film strip apparatus in every
school. It is not necessary to insist that visual aids to education
should be a state monopoly. On the other hand it is essential
not to hand the whole box of tricks exclusively to private
enterprise ; for if the profit-motive is uppermost there will
be a natural tendency to make only those sort of films which
will be widely used (elementary geography is an example)
while equally important subjects such as advanced chemistry
might be neglected because the number of students would be
much smaller.

Furthermore, the cost of installing the apparatus will in
most countries fall on the state, which will, therefore, have
a compulsive interest in its use.

On the other hand it is possible to envisage a situation in
which a state subsidy for projection apparatus will create a

profitable market for some types of educational films, thus guaranteeing the speculative producer against loss. As the projector-manufacturers may be financially tied-up with the film-producers and film-distributors, the overall benefit from state subsidy would be equivalent to having one's cake and eating it.

Thus, for educational films, a dual system would be the best, with government and private enterprise working together on an agreed plan. The one essential would be for the Ministry of Education, in consultation with local authorities, to be the planning centre.

If the state does its duty by the educational use of film and other visual aids, much more incentive will be given to commercial organisations and industries (such as existing patrons like Shell and I.C.I.) to make a greater contribution, which will be in addition both to the film programmes sponsored by the Government and to those put in hand by new companies who will no longer be deterred by the fear of insufficient distribution.

III. WORLD CINEMA.

Today the world of film is a world in transition. It reflects our wider world in its confusion of politics, economics, philosophy, and social relations.

If the value to mankind of this great medium of expression is to be fully developed, it must be through a complete re-assessment of the role of film, and this must be on an international scale. We must think about film in the same way as we are trying to think about food and reconstruction and finance ; that is, we must think in terms of the actual needs of people on a completely international level.

Taking the film industry as a whole, one may observe, with such international ideas in mind, a paradoxical situation.

On the one hand you find the film as an example of economic nationalism. It is one of the United States major industries both at home and for export. As far as export is concerned it is profitable on two levels—the obvious cash level and the almost equally obvious level which is summed up in the well-known American phrase ' A foot of film is worth a dollar's worth of trade '—or, in other words, American films condition people to the American goods they see in them.

These considerations hold good for Britain too, and the Government attitude to the British Film Industry today is largely conditioned by dollar-sterling relationships and, of course, the Marshall Plan.

On the other hand it is equally true that a healthy indigenous film industry is a necessity in the modern state. A country's films should be essentially national in style and spirit ; if they are they will be able to make a much stronger contribution to the international scene than if, as might easily happen, they came from the no-man's land of sterile cosmopolitanism.

Screen-space For All.

From the point of view of the film-maker, and of the audience, the whole question boils down to a reasonable share of world screen-space being available to all producing countries.

The American film has, as we have seen, dominated world screens hitherto. How far the United States can, or dare, maintain this monopoly is now questionable. Not merely Britain, but every country which realises the power of film is concerned to protect and enlarge its own film industry's activities. The greater awareness of propaganda which now exists as a result of World War II is causing many countries to watch ever more carefully the effect of American films on the consciousness of their own populace. Conversely, many countries (particularly those with little or no film production of their own), while wishing Hollywood to make films about themselves, are now more and more inclined to be sensitive as to how Hollywood handles and presents such films.

British Bargaining Point.
The British position at the moment is a key one, if only because government policy, for reasons already stated, makes it so. It is, by the way, worth remembering that championship of British films has not been a signal quality of Wardour Street, since both the distributors and exhibitors have for years done very well out of American films, and are to a considerable degree financially linked with American companies. In past years it was not simply the low reputation of British films which made life difficult for British producers, but also, and to a great measure, the discouragement found by even the best of them at the hands of the Wardour Street middlemen.

Today the increased quality and quantity of British films is not the only advantage. Equally important is the fact that the Government itself wants to back their circulation on an international scale. It was perhaps unfortunate that the general economic situation made it impossible to turn the fact that the British market represents America's real profit margin into a bargaining point as strong as it should be. Nevertheless, the whole Import Tax episode was important and significant.

Of course none of this alters the fact that British films will not be box office successes in the United States unless they are the sort of films which Americans enjoy. On the other hand this is something which can only be discovered if Americans

over a wide area have the chance of seeing a number of films
from Britain.   Hence Mr. Rank's drive for distribution deals
in the U.S.A.

The End of Ballyhoo.

The final answer for any country, and particularly for the
United States and Britain, can only be found in a revision of
the attitude of the Film Industry itself.

Hitherto the international circulation of films has been
carried out on a straight salesmanship basis—differing little,
if at all, from the methods employed in selling stockings
or chocolate.   But, unlike stockings, films are not just saleable
commodities, they are also conveyers of ideas—good, bad
or indifferent.   This has not been entirely ignored by the
industry, for the sales resistance which arises when a film
offends the moral or political susceptibilities of peoples or of
influential groups, is something which must be countered.
Hence the voluntary moral codes and self-censorships which
are such a curious facet of the film trade.

But on the whole these points have only been met on the
lower levels, those concerned mainly with the preservation
of a commercial market.

Today film magnates and corporations must face up to
a new approach to international distribution, an approach
which must look beyond the sales problem to other problems
which are concerned with relationships between peoples
and nations and based on common interests and common
needs.

Films, as carriers of ideas, have inevitably an increasing
political significance.   The film-man and the statesman can
no longer go their separate ways.   The relations between
Sir Stafford Cripps and Mr. Rank indicate a closer appreciation
of this than has hitherto been observed in the United States.

The time has come, indeed, for the salesman to be super-
seded.   The world of film has become a sensitively-balanced
world, and the old, crude, methods will upset the balance.
Knowledge and understanding of the international scene is
essential, and these have to go far beyond the techniques of
buying and selling.

Film industries today need to have ' Their own institutes of international affairs through which, continuously, producers, directors and writers can study the relationship of their films to the wider and more difficult world in which they now operate.' (John Grierson.)

This cannot be avoided by film people. It is a point of view which equates the buying and selling aspect with the ideological aspect. The content of a film is now a far more potent sales-factor than ever before. To make movies on the assumption that people don't want to think and are content with the superficial or the vapid is no longer a sane policy. For people *are* thinking, questioning, discussing, and restlessly reaching out for new things and new relationships. If the commercial film industry does not realise this point its financial structure will suffer, simply because it will have failed to follow the popular trend. An unselfish and imaginative attitude to current problems of box office is likely to pay off. Conversely, a retreat to the old, blind-as-a-bat conservative levels of ballyhoo and commercial-travellerdom will be fatal.

Film people may find a clarification of this thesis by studying the film world outside the cinemas—the non-theatrical world.

Propaganda—Real or Unreal ?

Here the prime consideration is not direct money-making, but the circulation of ideas and the fulfilment of needs.

The circulation of ideas involves the question of propaganda, but that is something which needs a book to itself and can only be briefly referred to here.

The reference is mainly to the fact that—as this country in particular discovered during World War II—the old conception of blatant, tub-thumping propaganda is outdated (if indeed it ever worked). The most successful film propaganda of the war was to be seen in films exported from Britain which were designed solely to report to Allied countries on progress and experiments made here in relation to problems common to all. Such films were not designed to tell others how wonderful we were. They were made to the thesis that it was right and proper for one country to make records of

its own achievements from which the other countries could
usefully benefit.

In other words these films were about things national
which were also things international. Under war pressure
we had made great strides in matters such as rationing,
nutrition, child-welfare, psychiatry, plastic surgery, and
labour-management relations. Our experience in these fields
was welcomed by other countries because they too were
deeply concerned in the same problems. Thus propaganda
became positive and not negative. The films were good
propaganda for Britain because they were not designed to
sell Britain or British ideas but rather to place British
experience freely at the disposal of others.

They belonged in fact to the truly international world in
which artificial barriers mean nothing in face of the reality
of common problems and common needs.

' Shop.'

On a world basis, therefore, it may be concluded that international discourse through non-theatrical film rests really on
the universality of ' shop.'

The development of the documentary film was profoundly
influenced by the realisation that shop knows no real international barriers. Just as at home films were not designed
for an amorphous general public, but for groups of citizenry
united by special interests, so, on a world basis, the unity of
special interests also held good.

Originally this thesis was, curiously enough, rammed home
by, of all people, philatelists.

A film was made about the design and production of the
George V Jubilee stamp, and it included some shots (in
colour) of the King's own stamp collection. It was not
a very good film but it was the first film ever made about
stamps

No sooner was its existence known than the G.P.O. Film
Unit (which had made the film) was bombarded with letters
and cables from individual stamp-collectors and philatelists'
associations all over the world. They wanted copies of the
film and they wanted them quick. In other words, stamp-

collectors are the same the world over whatever their language, race or creed.

It is but a short step from this internationale of hobbies to the internationale of jobs. The biologists and the chemists, the coalminers and the industrial designers, the truck-drivers and the doctors, the farmers and the professors, the teachers and the engineers—all are linked by their own special interests, regardless of their local habitation or their racial and national characteristics.

To intrude a personal reminiscence, I had in the Autumn of 1946 the interesting experience of making a brief lecture tour of Greece, Palestine and Egypt at the invitation of the British Council. Two things were impressive. Firstly, the most successful types of films being shown were ' shop ' films. A series on the Technique of Anaesthesia (sponsored incidentally by I.C.I.) was being warmly welcomed as a most valuable adjunct to hospital training and was, as a result, doing the name of Britain a thousand times more good than all the pretty pictures of Lifeguards or Stratford which were part of an earlier and now abandoned film policy.

Secondly, a lecture on the use of films in education, given in Jerusalem at a time of turmoil and political tension, brought together into one hall an audience of Jews and Arabs on a basis of complete amity. They were all teachers, and in the name of education they were united by common interests and purposes.

This is the real international world, the world of the technician, the agriculturalist, the scientist, the teacher and the artist. It is to this world that the film can and must make its greatest contribution.

Brass Tacks Before Utopia.

This conception extends even deeper, into the area of essential human needs. Every human being needs food, work, home and hope. Here identity of interest is absolute and universal. Here the world is already united by ties transcending all customs barriers, fortifications, language difficulties and diplomatic hush-hush. Here indeed is a world for film.

We are faced today with the problem of ensuring the widespread and continuous use of film on these urgent international levels. And here I emphasise once again the universality of the moving picture which has no language barriers and is readily understood by those who cannot read.

This problem of world film use is closely connected with the function and development of the United Nations and its specialised agencies such as the Food and Agriculture Organisation, The International Labour Office and, more particularly Unesco.

Approaching the United Nations concept in a down-to-earth manner, and avoiding vague idealisms and ' blueprints for Utopia,' we can immediately see a vast field of endeavour in which the film can play a most important part.

It is not a question of putting up a vast international production unit, with a variegated and polyglot staff, as some enthusiasts have suggested.

It is, rather, a question of mobilising the film-making capacity of each country within its proper and local terms, so that each may make its own contribution to the common pool. Further, it is a question of motivating an absolutely free flow of films of information and films of ideas all over the world. Freedom of expression means access to the means of expression.

It is axiomatic that these purposes, like all international purposes, cannot be achieved without the goodwill of the states members. It is equally axiomatic that goodwill arises most easily from self-interest. This is a particularly important point today, when so much of Europe, Asia and the Far East is desolated, and urgent problems of reconstruction and rehabilitation are uppermost in men's minds.

The Biggest Plan of All.

In this connection the programme to which Unesco is working in relation to the mass media of communation (press, radio, films) is highly encouraging.

It is a purely functional programme. It aims at meeting immediate needs in an immediate way. It throws the responsibility of assisting the ' Have Not ' nations fairly and squarely on the shoulders of the ' Have ' nations. It puts first things first, and is not concerned to fill Jugo Slavian schools with film projectors until it has been discovered whether Jugo Slavian schools have any roofs on them, and whether the classrooms have desks and blackboards and pencils and paper, and whether the children have clothes and shoes and food. It observes the rules of two-way traffic, and notes that the mass media could also be used to depict the plight of Jugo Slavian school-children to peoples of countries with surplus wealth. Financially, it accepts the plain thesis of the interdependence of world agencies. Its own terms of reference—Education, Science, Culture—mingle in a hundred different ways with the Food and Agricultural Organisation, the International Labour Office, the International Refugee Organisation and the rest.

If the initials Unesco are still a mystery to many, there need be no mystery about its job which, it is now clear, is nothing more or less than a *World Education Programme*— the first coherent plan for world education to be drawn up. Here we are concerned with film, but it is to be noted that much of the plan is based on the working together of all the mass media. Thus it is impossible to consider the film plan without taking count of the press and radio plans ; for the purposes to be served are identical.

Briefly put, the plan is, first, to create the physical circumstances throughout the world under which the constructive use of the mass media can be carried out; second, long term projects for the use and interchange of mass-media material.

The first part of the plan is concerned with the rehabilitation of countries hard hit by the war, and with bringing into full action the resources of countries more luckily placed ; it is concerned, too, with the encouragement and development of fundamental education in all those vast areas such as China, Africa, and South America, where the means of education have been lacking for centuries, war or no war.

Facts come first. It is necessary to find out what specific shortages exist in deficiency countries, in terms of raw film, projectors, cameras and, not least, skilled technicians. Then the ' Have ' countries must come to the rescue. Not only must they supply the missing equipment, but they must also open their doors to people whom the deficiency countries want to send for expert training in the production and use of films.

Next comes a survey of existing obstacles to the free flow of ideas—things like copyright restrictions, suppression or distortion of ideas, and the whole field of censorship.

There is already in existence a convention designed to free from Customs duties all films and other visual media which are of an Educational, Scientific and Cultural nature. Without the full ratification of this convention by all countries the free flow of films of information and enlightenment will be strangled. Not only must it be ratified but also the certifying of educational and scientific and cultural films must be carried out in an exceptionally generous spirit. It must always be done with the idea that ' more ' is better than ' fewer.' In all countries where they exist groups and organisations concerned with the use of such films will have to exert their own influence on governments to ensure that the purpose of the convention is implemented to the full.

Finally there is the pooling of information, and the creation of efficient machinery for the interchange of knowledge of and about films between producers and users in all countries.

Here two things are needed. In the first place there must be the right sort of organisation within each country, such as Institutes of Scientific Information and, very importantly, National Visual Councils, whose job it will be to provide a service of films to all community organisations and groups which make use of cinema. In this country a national foundation for visual aids has, in fact, already been established.

These Councils will be able, through their community contacts, to focus the film needs of the groups in their own country, and to express them both to local producers and to Unesco itself, which will act as an International Clearing House for all information about films, film strips and other visual material.

This Clearing House idea is one of the main keys to any international film project. It can ensure that all countries adopt the same methods of collecting and cataloguing information. It can supply each country with full and up-to-date film information collected from all other countries. It can thereby be in a position of knowing at any given moment *on a world scale* what particular gaps there are, and inform film-makers in various countries what new films are needed to fill these gaps.

Unesco has of course a number of difficulties to surmount. Its budget is minuscule. At the time of writing a number of nations are not members of it, amongst them the Soviet Union, without whose full co-operation no world-scheme can satisfactorily operate. And in any case, like any functional organisation, it depends on the backing, goodwill, enthusiasm, and practical help both in finance and in mind, of its members. If it fails it will be because nations have not played their part. Whatever happens nothing will alter the fact that a world plan for film must be put into full operation if this great medium is to play its part in bringing the peoples of the world closer together in mutual understanding—the only real guarantee against war.

We can see therefore a twofold path towards world cinema.

On the one hand there is the major international idea— freedom of expression and therefore free access to the means of expression. This means the abandonment of a chauvanist attitude towards the problems of production and distribution. It means a reconsideration by the Americans of their whole position, and an eventual giving-up—willingly rather than by force of events—of their long-established world-monopoly. It means—and this will not happen without American goodwill —that other countries must jettison their restrictive quotas, financial embargos, and political censorships. It means, too that countries with existing production facilities must freely assist countries which as yet have no film industries, but which are seeking, whether for purposes of education or entertainment, or both, to establish them.

On the other hand there is the direct contribution to world cinema which can only come effectively from the quality of national production. We have already seen that the best films reflect the nature and the character of the country which

produces them. Creative film-makers in each country must
acquire a wide vision in this matter, so that the subject-matter
and treatment of their films meet world as well as local needs.
Here it may well prove that commercial considerations
are identifiable with international ideals.

Of course none of this precludes a measure of internationally-
organised production. During the last years of the war we
saw in *The True Glory* a fascinating and wholly successful
job of collaboration between British and American film-
workers.

But I am sure that for many years to come the national
contribution will be the most important. No better example
of this could be found at this stage than Rossellini's great
film *Paisa*—a film in three languages dealing with the inter-
relationships, under circumstances of dreadful violence,
between Italians, British, Americans and Germans, but
emphasising all the time the fundamentals of human dealings,
both good and evil. Like *The Last Chance*, *Paisa* is wholly
international while at the same time it is in all creative aspects
wholly and properly national.

We need, more than ever before, the freest possible flow
of all means of cultural expression between the nations.
The answer to this problem can, in my opinion, only be found
in the quality and content of the films themselves. For
instance, the difficulties of Hollywood arise chiefly because
the Hollywood film-makers have not kept up with the times.
They do not think deeply enough about the needs and the
moods of people in other countries. They do not care enough
about what is going on outside America. If their films are
less successful that is not because they are American, but
because they do not satisfy the current needs of their
audiences.

The same problem exists in Britain. The rapid rise of the
British film industry under Mr. Rank will not continue unless,
in the standard and content of the films we make, we take
full account of factors other than the more old-fashioned
conceptions of ' box-office.'

We are, in fact, all in the same boat. The free circulation
of films all over the world will not come about until we all

realise that our film-making must be conditioned by two main considerations—first, a respect for the culture of other countries, and second, the fact that the trading relations between countries must be based on the idea of giving as well as taking.

These are examples of the attitude which must be taken if we are to build up a free exchange of films throughout the world on the basis of mutual respect for our various cultures and achievements.

But if this is true of the entertainment film, it is equally true of all the other uses of film. Films outside the cinemas can be subject to the same sanctions as the films of entertainment inside the cinemas. The only difference is that films of information and enlightenment are more likely from the start to put forward the point of view needed.

But even if we are so rash as to take the most optimistic view of the present world situation regarding the free flow of every sort of film, there is another point, of the most vital importance, which we must consider. It is this.

We agree for the need to use the film to express, shall we say, the liberty, equality and fraternity of men. But what in fact do men *need* if they are to express their fraternity, establish their equality, and secure their liberty ?

Millions of people in the world do not have the slightest opportunity to see films, let alone make them. Consider the conditions not only in some of the devastated countries of Europe, but also in Africa, China and South America. How can we really talk about the free flow of ideas or the free flow of films when one single film projector for one single village in China or Africa costs as much as $500 ? Again, how can we talk of the free expression of culture and achievement when so many countries lack not only the apparatus, but also the skills and techniques of film-making ? If some countries have the skills, the machinery and the finance for film-making, and others do not, one can hardly be surprised if suspicions exist regarding the imposition of cultural and other ideas by one country on another. The free flow of films will only be achieved when all people have access to the making and the use of films. This means that plans for the manufacture of film projectors, for instance, must be laid on such a scale that their cost is a practical proposition in China and Africa as well as in the wealthier areas of the world. It means that opportunities must be provided to people from all over the world to get training in the production and use of films, as for instance through the important fellowship schemes which have already been instituted by Unesco. The importance of all this can be seen merely in considering how much the film can do in one field alone, that of fundamental education in less advanced countries ; for this includes the fight against illiteracy, in which, as we have seen, the film can play perhaps the most important role of all.

We in Britain, because of our pioneer work in this field, can do as much as, if not more than any other country. It is not only that we can, by serving our own needs, serve the needs of others (our stake in world multilateral trade alone should ensure this), but also that in such things as colonial development (now better named trusteeship) we can, by a wise and far-seeing approach to fundamental education in an area like Africa, make a profound contribution to deficiency countries everywhere.

For behind all the abstract words like nations, governments, states, sovereignties, lies the obvious but often forgotten fact that they all mean people. People are more important than anything else in the world ; and in seeking, as all do, as all must, the good life, they are at one with one another wherever they live, and whatever their social, economic and cultural conditions.

We cannot know everything all the time. We cannot be everywhere all the time. But universal knowledge—the Wellsian world-brain—is not beyond our realisation. And the film, with all its cogency and clarity, *can* be everywhere all the time.

THE END

BIBLIOGRAPHY

(A selected list from the many books about films.
Books of special value are marked with an asterisk)

(a) Books.

ADLER, MORTIMER—*Art and Prudence* (Longmans Green, New York, 1937).

AGATE, JAMES—*Around Cinemas* (Home & Van Thal, 1946)

ANONYMOUS—**The Factual Film* (*Arts Enquiry*) (P.E.P. and Oxford University Press, 1947).

ARNHEIM, RUDOLPH—*Film* (Faber & Faber, 1933).

AROSSEV, A. (Ed.)—*Soviet Cinema* (Voks, 1934).

BAECHLIN, PETER—**Histoire Economique du Cinéma* (Paris, 1947).

BALCON, MICHAEL with LINDGREN, HARDY and MANVELL—*Twenty Years Of British Films* (Falcon, 1947).

BARDECHE, M. and BRASSILACH, R.—**History Of The Film* (Allen & Unwin, 1938).

BARRY, IRIS—*Let's Go To The Pictures* (Chatto & Windus, 1926).

BELFRAGE, CEDRIC—*The Promised Land* (Gollancz, 1939).

BENOIT-LEVY, JEAN—**Les Grandes Missions Du Cinéma* (Parizeau, Montreal, 1944).

BETTS, ERNEST—*Heraclitus* (Kegan Paul, 1928).

BIRD, JOHN H.—*Cinema Parade* (Cornish, 1947).

BLAKESTON, OSWALD (Ed.)—*Working for The Films* (Focal Press, 1947).

BLUMER, HERBERT—*Movies And Conduct* (Macmillan, New York, 1933).

BOWER, DALLAS—*Plan For Cinema* (Dent, 1936).

BRUNEL, ADRIAN—*Film Production* (Newnes, 1936).

BRYHER—*Film Problems Of Soviet Russia* (Territet, Switzerland, 1929).

BUCHANAN, ANDREW—*Films : The Way Of The Cinema* (Pitman, 1932) ; *The Art Of Film Production* (Pitman, 1936) ; *Films And The Future* (Allen & Unwin, 1945) ; *Going To The Cinema* (Phoenix, 1947).

BURNFORD, PAUL—*Filming for Amateurs* (Pitman, 1946).

CAMERON, A. C. (Ed.)—**The Film In National Life* (Allen & Unwin, 1932).

CAMERON, KEN—**Sound And The Documentary Film* (Pitman, 1947).

CARRICK, EDWARD—*Designing For Motion Pictures* (Studio, 1941).

CARTER, HUNTLY—*The New Spirit In The Cinema* (Shaylor, 1930).

CHARENSOL, G.—*Panorama du Cinéma* (Paris, 1929).

COOKE, ALASTAIR (Ed.)—*Garbo and The Nightwatchmen* (Cape, 1937).

DALE, EDGAR—**How To Appreciate Motion Pictures* (Macmillan, New York, 1933) ; **The Content Of Motion Pictures* (Macmillan, New York, 1935).

DANISCHEWSKY, M. (Ed.)—*Michael Balcon's 25 years in Films* (World Film Publications, 1947).

DAVY, CHARLES (Ed.)—*Footnotes To The Film* (Lovat Dickson, 1938).

DELLUC, LOUIS—*Cinéma et Cie* (Paris, 1920) ; *Charlie Chaplin* (Lane, 1922).

DRINKWATER, JOHN—*The Life and Adventures of Carl Laemmle* (Heinemann, 1931).

DURDEN, J. V. see SMITH, PERCY.

EDUCATION, BOARD OF—*Handbook Of Suggestions For Teachers* (H.M.S.O. 1937).

ELLIOTT, ERIC—*Anatomy Of Motion Picture Art* (Pool, 1928).

ELLIOTT, W. F.—*Sound Recording For Films* (Pitman, 1937).

EISENSTEIN, S. M.—*The Film Sense* (Faber & Faber, 1943).

ERNST, MORRIS—*The First Freedom* (Macmillan, New York, 1946).

ERNST, MORRIS with LORENTZ PARE—*Censored* (Cape & Smith, New York, 1930).

FAIRTHORNE, R.—see LEGG, STUART.

FIELD, MARY, with SMITH, PERCY—*Secrets Of Nature* (Faber & Faber, 1934)—see also under SMITH, PERCY.

FORD, RICHARD—*Children At The Cinema* (Allen & Unwin, 1939).

GEORGE, W. H.—*The Cinema In The School* (Pitman, 1935).

GOLDWYN, SAMUEL—*Behind The Screen* (Doran, New York, 1923).

GRIERSON, JOHN—see HARDY, H. FORSYTH.

GRIFFITH, Mrs. D. W.—*When The Movies Were Young* (Dutton, New York, 1925).

HAMPTON, BENJAMIN—*A History Of The Movies* (Covici-Friede, New York, 1931).

HARDY, H. FORSYTH (Ed.)—*Grierson On Documentary* (Collins, 1946) see also BALCON, MICHAEL.

HUETTIG, MAE C.—*Economic Control Of The Motion Picture Industry* (University of Pennsylvania, 1944).

HUNTER, WILLIAM—*Scrutiny Of Cinema* (Wishart, 1932).

HUNTLEY, JOHN—*British Film Music* (Skelton Robinson, 1947).

INGLIS, RUTH—*Freedom for The Movies* (University of Chicago, 1947).

JACOBS, LEWIS—*The Rise Of The American Film* (Harcourt Brace, New York, 1940).

JUNGE, H.—*Plan For Film Studios* (Focal Press, London & New York, 1945).

KLEIN, A. B.—*Colour Cinematography* (Chapman & Hall, 1937).

KLINGENDER, F. D.—see LEGG, STUART.

KNOWLES, DOROTHY—*The Censor, The Drama, and The Film* (Allen & Unwin, 1934).

KRACAUER, SIEGFRIED—*From Caligari to Hitler* (Dennis Dobson, 1947).

LAMBERT, R. S. (Ed.)—*For Filmgoers Only* (Faber & Faber, 1934).

LATHAM, G.—see NOTCUTT, L.

LAUWERYS, J. A. (Ed.)—*The Film In The School* (Christophers, 1935).

LAWS, FREDERICK (Ed.)—*Made For Millions* (Contact Press, 1947).

LEGG, STUART and FAIRTHORNE, R.—*Cinema and Television* (Longmans Green, 1939).

LEGG, STUART and KLINGENDER, F. D.—*Money Behind The Screen* (Lawrence & Wishart, 1937).

LEJEUNE, C. A.—*Cinema* (Maclehose, 1931) ;   *Chestnuts In Her Lap* (Phoenix Press, 1947).

LEONARD, HAROLD (Ed. for WPA)—*The Film Index* vol. i. (Museum of Modern Art, New York, 1941).

LINDGREN, ERNEST—see BALCON, MICHAEL.

LINDSAY, VACHEL—*The Art Of The Moving Picture* (Macmillan, New York, 1915).

LONDON, KURT—*Film Music* (Faber & Faber, 1936).

LORENTZ, PARE—see ERNST, MORRIS.

LUNATSCHARSKI—*Der Russische Revolutionsfilm* (Berlin, 1929).

MANVELL, ROGER—*Film* (Penguin Books, 1944 ; revised edition 1946) See also BALCON, MICHAEL.

MAYER, J. P.—*Sociology Of The Film* (Faber & Faber, 1947).

MIRAMS, GORDON—*Speaking Candidly* (Pauls, New Zealand, 1945)

MOLEY, RAYMOND—*The Hays Office* (Bobs Merrill, 1945)

MONTAGU, IVOR—*The Political Censorship Of Films* (Gollancz, 1929).

MOUSSINAC, LEON—*Le Cinéma Soviètique* (Paris, 1928) ;   *Panoramique Du Cinéma* (Paris, 1929).

MULLER, GOTTFRIED—*Dramaturgie Des Theaters Und Des Films* (Wurzburg, 1942).

NAUMBERG, NANCY (Ed.)—*We Make The Movies* (Faber & Faber, 1938).

NICOLL, ALLARDYCE—*Film and Theatre* (Harrap, 1936).

NILSEN, VLADIMIR—*The Cinema As A Graphic Art* (Newnes, 1936).

NOTCUTT, L. and LATHAM, G.—*The African and The Cinema* (Edinburgh House, 1937).

O'LAOGHAIRE, LIAM—*Invitation To The Film* (Kerryman, Eire, 1945).

PAUL, ELLIOTT and QUINTANILLA, LUIS—*With A Hays Nonny Nonny* (Random House, 1942).

PERLMAN, W. J.—*The Movies On Trial* (Macmillan, New York, 1936).

POWELL, DILYS—*Films Since 1939* (British Council, 1947).

POWELL, MICHAEL—*20,000 Feet On Foula* (Faber & Faber, 1938).

PUDOVKIN, V. I.—*Film Technique* (Newnes, 1933) ;   *Film Acting* (Newnes, 1935).

QUIGLEY, MARTIN—*Decency In Motion Pictures* (Macmillan, New York, 1937).

QUINTANILLA, LUIS—see PAUL, ELLIOTT.

RAMSAYE, TERRY—*A Million And One Nights* (Simon & Schuster, New York, 1926).

RICHTER, HANS—*Filmgegner Von Heute, Filmfreunde Von Morgen* (Berlin, 1929).

ROBSON, E. W. and M. M.—*The Film Answers Back* (The Bodley Head, 1939).

ROSTEN, LEO—*Hollywood* (Harcourt Brace, 1941).

ROTHA, PAUL—**The Film Till Now* (Cape, 1930) ; *Celluloid* (Longmans Green, 1931) ; **Documentary Film* (Faber & Faber, 1936 : revised edition, 1939) ; *Movie Parade* (Studio, 1936).

SADOUL, GEORGES—**L'Invention Du Cinéma* 1832-97 (Denoel, Paris, 1945) ; **Les Pionniers Du Cinéma* 1897-1910 (Denoel, Paris, 1947).

SELDES, GILBERT—**The Seven Lively Arts* (Harper, New York, 1924) ; *An Hour With The Movies And The Talkies* (Lippincott, Philadelphia, 1929) ; **Movies For The Million* (Batsford, 1937).

SINCLAIR, UPTON—*Upton Sinclair Presents William Fox* (Published by author, 1933).

SMITH, PERCY, with DURDEN, J. V. and FIELD, MARY—*Cine-Biology* (Penguin Books, 1941).

SPEARMAN and BURT—*The Cinema In Education* (Allen & Unwin, 1925).

SPENCER, D. A. with WALEY, H. D.—*The Cinema Today* (Oxford University Press, 1940).

SPOTTISWOODE, RAYMOND—*A Grammar Of The Film* (Faber & Faber, 1935).

STRASSER, ALEX—*Amateur Films* (Link House, 1936) ; *Amateur Movies* (Studio 1937 ; revised edition, 1947).

TALLENTS, Sir STEPHEN—**The Projection Of Britain* (Faber & Faber, 1932).

THORP, MARGARET F.—**America At The Movies* (Faber & Faber, 1946).

TYLER, PARKER—*Magic and Myth of The Movies* (Henry Holt, New York, 1947).

UNESCO—**Report of Technical Needs Commission* (Paris, 1947) and annually.

VEDRES, NICOLE—*Images du Cinéma Français* (Paris, 1945).

WALEY, H. D.—see SPENCER, D. A.

WAPLES, DONALD (Ed.)—*Print, Radio And Film In A Democracy* (University of Chicago, 1942).

WILSON, NORMAN—*Presenting Scotland* (Edinburgh Film Guild, 1945).

WOOD and FREEMAN—*Motion Pictures In The Classroom* (New York 1926).

WRIGLEY and LEYLAND—*The Cinema, Historical, Technical and Bibliographical* (Grafton, 1939).

ZWANZIGER, M.—*Function And Development Of The Cinema* (Haifa, Palestine, 1946).

(b) Reference.

British Film Year Book (British Yearbooks). *Informational Film Year Book* (Albyn Press, Edinburgh). *International Motion Picture Almanac* (Quigley Publications). *Kinematograph Year Book* (Odhams Press).

(c) Periodicals.

Amateur Cine World
*Cinema and Todays Cinema**
Cinema Quarterly†
Close-Up†
*Daily Film Renter**
Documentary Film News
Experimental Cinema†
*Film Industry**
Film Weekly
Home Movies

*Kinematograph Weekly**
*Motion Picture Herald**
Penguin Film Review
Picturegoer
Sequence
Sight And Sound
*16 Millimetre User**
*Variety**
World Film News†

†Ceased publication, but back numbers or bound volumes well worth study.

*Trade papers.

The Arno Press Cinema Program

THE LITERATURE OF CINEMA

Series I & II

American Academy of Political and Social Science. **The Motion Picture in Its Economic and Social Aspects**, edited by Clyde L. King. **The Motion Picture Industry**, edited by Gordon S. Watkins. *The Annals*, November, 1926/1927.

Agate, James. **Around Cinemas.** 1946.

Agate, James. **Around Cinemas. (Second Series).** 1948.

Balcon, Michael, Ernest Lindgren, Forsyth Hardy and Roger Manvell. **Twenty Years of British Film, 1925-1945.** 1947.

Bardèche, Maurice and Robert Brasillach. **The History of Motion Pictures,** edited by Iris Barry. 1938.

Benoit-Levy, Jean. **The Art of the Motion Picture.** 1946.

Blumer, Herbert. **Movies and Conduct.** 1933.

Blumer, Herbert and Philip M. Hauser. **Movies, Delinquency, and Crime.** 1933.

Buckle, Gerard Fort. **The Mind and the Film.** 1926.

Carter, Huntly. **The New Spirit in the Cinema.** 1930.

Carter, Huntly. **The New Spirit in the Russian Theatre, 1917-1928.** 1929.

Carter, Huntly. **The New Theatre and Cinema of Soviet Russia.** 1924.

Charters, W. W. **Motion Pictures and Youth.** 1933.

Cinema Commission of Inquiry. **The Cinema: Its Present Position and Future Possibilities.** 1917.

Dale, Edgar. **The Content of Motion Pictures.** 1935.

Dale, Edgar. **How to Appreciate Motion Pictures.** 1937.

Dale, Edgar. **Children's Attendance at Motion Pictures.** Dysinger, Wendell S. and Christian A. Ruckmick. **The Emotional Responses of Children to the Motion Picture Situation.** 1935.

Dale, Edgar, Fannie W. Dunn, Charles F. Hoban, Jr., and Etta Schneider. **Motion Pictures in Education: A Summary of the Literature.** 1938.

Davy, Charles. **Footnotes to the Film.** 1938.

Dickinson, Thorold and Catherine De la Roche. **Soviet Cinema.** 1948.

Dickson, W. K. L., and Antonia Dickson. **History of the Kinetograph, Kinetoscope and Kinetophonograph.** 1895.

Forman, Henry James. **Our Movie Made Children.** 1935.

Freeburg, Victor Oscar. **The Art of Photoplay Making.** 1918.

Freeburg, Victor Oscar. **Pictorial Beauty on the Screen.** 1923.

Hall, Hal, editor. **Cinematographic Annual,** 2 vols. 1930/1931.

Hampton, Benjamin B. **A History of the Movies.** 1931.

Hardy, Forsyth. **Scandinavian Film.** 1952.

Hepworth, Cecil M. **Animated Photography: The A B C of the Cinematograph.** 1900.

Hoban, Charles F., Jr., and Edward B. Van Ormer. **Instructional Film Research 1918-1950.** 1950.

Holaday, Perry W. and George D. Stoddard. **Getting Ideas from the Movies.** 1933.

Hopwood, Henry V. **Living Pictures.** 1899.

Hulfish, David S. **Motion-Picture Work.** 1915.

Hunter, William. **Scrutiny of Cinema.** 1932.

Huntley, John. **British Film Music.** 1948.

Irwin, Will. **The House That Shadows Built.** 1928.

Jarratt, Vernon. **The Italian Cinema.** 1951.

Jenkins, C. Francis. **Animated Pictures.** 1898.

Lang, Edith and George West. **Musical Accompaniment of Moving Pictures.** 1920.

L'Art Cinematographique, Nos. 1-8. 1926-1931.

London, Kurt. **Film Music.** 1936.

Lutz, E [dwin] G [eorge]. **The Motion-Picture Cameraman.** 1927.

Manvell, Roger. **Experiment in the Film.** 1949.

Marey, Etienne Jules. **Movement.** 1895.

Martin, Olga J. **Hollywood's Movie Commandments.** 1937.

Mayer, J. P. **Sociology of Film: Studies and Documents.** 1946. New Introduction by J. P. Mayer.

Münsterberg, Hugo. **The Photoplay: A Psychological Study.** 1916.

Nicoll, Allardyce. **Film and Theatre.** 1936.

Noble, Peter. **The Negro in Films.** 1949.

Peters, Charles C. **Motion Pictures and Standards of Morality.** 1933.

Peterson, Ruth C. and L. L. Thurstone. **Motion Pictures and the Social Attitudes of Children.** Shuttleworth, Frank K. and Mark A. May. **The Social Conduct and Attitudes of Movie Fans.** 1933.

Phillips, Henry Albert. **The Photodrama.** 1914.

Photoplay Research Society. **Opportunities in the Motion Picture Industry.** 1922.

Rapée, Erno. **Encyclopaedia of Music for Pictures.** 1925.

Rapée, Erno. **Motion Picture Moods for Pianists and Organists.** 1924.

Renshaw, Samuel, Vernon L. Miller and Dorothy P. Marquis. **Children's Sleep.** 1933.

Rosten, Leo C. **Hollywood: The Movie Colony, The Movie Makers.** 1941.

Sadoul, Georges. **French Film.** 1953.

Screen Monographs I, 1923-1937. 1970.

Screen Monographs II, 1915-1930. 1970.

Sinclair, Upton. **Upton Sinclair Presents William Fox.** 1933.

Talbot, Frederick A. **Moving Pictures.** 1912.

Thorp, Margaret Farrand. **America at the Movies.** 1939.

Wollenberg, H. H. **Fifty Years of German Film.** 1948.

RELATED BOOKS AND PERIODICALS

Allister, Ray. **Friese-Greene: Close-Up of an Inventor.** 1948.

Art in Cinema: A Symposium of the Avant-Garde Film, edited by Frank Stauffacher. 1947.

The Art of Cinema: Selected Essays. New Foreword by George Amberg. 1971.

Balázs, Béla. **Theory of the Film.** 1952.

Barry, Iris. **Let's Go to the Movies.** 1926.

de Beauvoir, Simone. **Brigitte Bardot and the Lolita Syndrome.** 1960.

Carrick, Edward. **Art and Design in the British Film.** 1948.

Close Up. Vols. 1-10, 1927-1933 (all published).

Cogley, John. **Report on Blacklisting. Part I: The Movies.** 1956.

Eisenstein, S. M. **Que Viva Mexico!** 1951.

Experimental Cinema. 1930-1934 (all published).

Feldman, Joseph and Harry. **Dynamics of the Film.** 1952.

Film Daily Yearbook of Motion Pictures. Microfilm, 18 reels,
  35 mm. 1918-1969.

Film Daily Yearbook of Motion Pictures. 1970.

Film Daily Yearbook of Motion Pictures. (Wid's Year Book).
  3 vols., 1918-1922.

The Film Index: A Bibliography. Vol. I: The Film as Art. 1941.

Film Society Programmes. 1925-1939 (all published).

Films: A Quarterly of Discussion and Analysis. Nos. 1-4, 1939-1940
  (all published).

Flaherty, Frances Hubbard. **The Odyssey of a Film-Maker:
  Robert Flaherty's Story.** 1960.

General Bibliography of Motion Pictures, edited by Carl Vincent,
  Riccardo Redi, and Franco Venturini. 1953.

Hendricks, Gordon. **Origins of the American Film.** 1961-1966. New
  Introduction by Gordon Hendricks.

Hound and Horn: Essays on Cinema, 1928-1934. 1971.

Huff, Theodore. **Charlie Chaplin.** 1951.

Kahn, Gordon. **Hollywood on Trial.** 1948.

New York Times Film Reviews, 1913-1968. 1970.

Noble, Peter. **Hollywood Scapegoat: The Biography of Erich
  von Stroheim.** 1950.

Robson, E. W. and M. M. **The Film Answers Back.** 1939.

Weinberg, Herman G., editor. **Greed.** 1971.

Wollenberg, H. H. **Anatomy of the Film.** 1947.

Wright, Basil. **The Use of the Film.** 1948.